HID
—i
HISTORY

MW00576482

The Untold Stories of

Women During the Industrial Revolution

By Danielle Thorne

HIDDEN IN HISTORY: THE UNTOLD STORIES OF WOMEN DURING THE INDUSTRIAL REVOLUTION

1405 SW 6th Avenue • Ocala, Florida 34471 • Phone 352-622-1825 • Fax 352-622-1875
Website: www.atlantic-pub.com • Email: sales@atlantic-pub.com
SAN Number: 268-1250

Library of Congress Cataloging-in-Publication Data

Names: Thorne, Danielle, author.

Title: The untold stories of women during the Industrial Revolution / by Danielle Thorne.

Description: Ocala, Fla. : Atlantic Publishing Group, Inc., 2019. | Series: Hidden in history | Includes bibliographical references and index. |

Identifiers: LCCN 2018058904 (print) | LCCN 2018060268 (ebook) | ISBN 9781620236376 (ebook) | ISBN 9781620236369 (alk. paper) | ISBN 1620236362 (alk.paper)

Subjects: LCSH: Women employees--United States--History. | Women inventors--United States--History. | Industrial revolution--United States--History.

Classification: LCC HD6055.6.U6 (ebook) | LCC HD6055.6.U6 .T46 2019 (print) |DDC 331.4092/520973--dc23

LC record available at https://lccn.loc.gov/2018058904

Printed in the United States

PROJECT MANAGER: Danielle Lieneman
INTERIOR LAYOUT AND JACKET DESIGN: Nicole Sturk

Over the years, we have adopted a number of dogs from rescues and shelters. First there was Bear and after he passed, Ginger and Scout. Now, we have Kira, another rescue. They have brought immense joy and love not just into our lives, but into the lives of all who met them.

We want you to know a portion of the profits of this book will be donated in Bear, Ginger and Scout's memory to local animal shelters, parks, conservation organizations, and other individuals and nonprofit organizations in need of assistance.

– Douglas & Sherri Brown,
President & Vice-President of Atlantic Publishing

Table of Contents

There is a ticking timepiece shaped like a kitten. It has shiny brass gears and a golden tail that swishes back and forth and back and forth ... until a small explosion of steam bursts out of its mouth with a hiss.

Mary wakes up with a jerk. It was just a dream. She hears the sounds of her parents getting dressed in the next room of their tiny company apartment. She climbs out of bed in the dark and, with a shiver, pulls a wool dress over her head and ties on an apron. A small pair of sturdy clogs wait for her tired feet. Luckily, she has her mother's old shawl to keep her warm until the sun comes up, or until she walks through the factory doors. It's 4:30 in the morning, and 13-year-old Mary has slept less than six hours.

After a quick bite of breakfast — a piece of cold bread and a sip of almost sour milk — she follows her father, mother, and older brothers outside, and they walk as a family toward the loud, smoking factory buildings at the company mill that turns wool into thread. Mary's little sister Hannah turned 10 years old recently and is now old enough to stay home with the babies while the rest of the family toils in the factory six days a week.

The entrance gate is the only place they are allowed to enter the factory, and they hurry along with Mother's instructions to take their small lunches, a warning to be careful ringing in their ears. They cannot afford any more injuries. Jonah was stabbed by one of the steel points of the automatic looms last year, and it cost a small fortune to take him to a doctor. He almost died.

The warning bell rings, and Mary rushes to her place in line among the machinery for the start bell at 6:30 a.m. The work day is run by bells, and they start banging them as early as 5:00 a.m. Later, there will be a noon day signal where everyone will stop and walk outside to the yard for some weak tea, and perhaps bread if they are lucky, and then they will return to work until the dinner break at 6:30 that night. Some seasons they work after a dinner of potatoes and bacon until much later; other times they are happy to be finished by 8:00 p.m.

It doesn't matter that it's only springtime; it's hot and stuffy inside. The dirty windows don't let in much light, and the bosses keep them closed up to stop the threads from blowing around. Sometimes, dust and tiny float-ing pieces of cotton in the air get caught in Mary's throat and make her cough until her lungs hurt.

Mary listens hard and tries to focus on her job as she walks along the busy lines watching for broken threads. Even though there are constant rattling and humming noises from the steam powered machines, she must pay close attention — she is a **piecer**. The younger children replace empty **bobbins**, or spools of thread, but Mary's job is to lean over the spinning machines and fix any threads that break. It's dangerous work. She could have her skin scraped to the bone, lose a finger, or fall in and have her body mangled up into the machinery until she is quite dead.

When the bell for her 20-minute break rings at noon, Mary feels exhausted. Her feet and fingers ache. She hopes to see her friends or mother and maybe find something extra to eat. A sweet would be nice! She's too tired to play with the younger children running about the yard between their duties. She does not have the money to buy a book — not yet. There isn't much money for toys or books, or cute, fancy hats. But someday Mary will be older and more experienced.

If she's lucky, Mary could be hired as one of the older factory girls, like her mother once was, and live in a boarding house. On her own, she could make enough money to take care of herself until she can become a teacher. If she saves her wages and finds a way to go to school, she could move far away from the city's mills and into the country, where the sun shines bright, the breeze smells like flowers, and there are no bells, machines, or steaming smokestacks calling everyone to work night and day.

Mary remembers her dream about the shiny, moving kitten machine and sighs. She'd rather have a real one — one that does not steam or hiss or smell like oil and wool.

Chapter One

Revolution

Across The Pond

*S*teampunk. *Victorian. The Age of the Machines.* If you've ever read a book or seen a movie described as "steampunk" or any of those other words, it probably took place during a period of history known as the **Industrial Revolution**.

Originating in Great Britain during the middle of the 1700s, the Industrial Revolution was the era of modern-day inventions. This time period includes steam-powered machines and fantastic scientific discoveries that used natural resources and ingenuity to create the modern marvels of the day. Besides amazing automatic weaving looms and roaring locomotives, even simple, everyday timekeepers became pocket watches, and little dolls became functional and amazing robots called **automatons**.

 Sherlock Holmes is the brilliant, clever detective made famous in the books and short stories of Sir Author Conan Doyle. The detective and his sidekick, Dr. Watson, live and vanquish their foes, including some women, during the era of the Industrial Revolution.

The country of Great Britain had the perfect ingredients to create a new age: a lot of new and old money, rich natural resources, millions of citizens who needed work, and a powerful Royal Navy to protect trade ships that could sail around the globe to deliver silk dresses or coal. The Industrial Revolution would last about 100 years into the middle of the 19th Century and spread around the world.

As scientists and innovative thinkers began to invent wonderful machines and **patent** them, those with property and wealth invested their money into businesses. There wasn't room to run big machines and hire workers in houses, so large, enclosed buildings called **manufactories**, or factories, were built to house them all.

 A patent is a document that gives a creator or inventor the individual right to a creation that no one else can copy, use, or sell. A patented invention means no one else can produce it without permission, and must pay a royalty fee if they do, until the patent deadline expires. Most patents in the United States today are for 20 years.

Artisans, or craftsmen like shoemakers and dressmakers, left their home businesses to work in manufactories. People working land that wasn't their own moved their families to cities in hopes of better pay. Women and children, who had always labored beside men in agriculture or artisan work, found that they could be hired, too. It was not a great deal of money when compared to the danger and hard labor expected, but it provided food, shelter, and, if one was fortunate, enough money to buy an education.

As Great Britain began to produce clothing more easily and mine coal more quickly, money flowed through society, and instead of people being just rich and poor, a middle class developed. These working citizens began to notice the **inequality** around them as some men were paid more and given easier jobs. Women began to fight for the rights of their own sex and for the safety of children. These sometimes violent protests led to the formation of **unions**, or groups organized by workers to mediate with company managers and owners for fair treatment.

The Industrial Revolution was born and, with time, would spread like a brushfire across the English Channel into Europe and then across the pond to the United States of America.

The old ways

For century after century, the basic needs of the world were met by farmers who grew food and raised livestock, and by craftsmen who made clothing, shoes, pottery, and just about everything else by hand. Traditions and these important skills were passed down from one family to another, and so, from villages to towns, these handmade goods were traded and sold. This time of **domestic manufacture** is defined as a period between the mid-1300s up to around 1750.

Life in England, Europe, Russia, and colonial America often included a small family garden or farm alongside the family trade. An entire family of craftsmen could produce shoes, rugs, carpets, wool, cloth, or even furniture. This rustic type of manufacturing was labeled the **cottage industry**.

Soon, the family business wasn't the only way goods were produced. Communities formed relationships between masters and apprentices. A master was a man who knew his trade. An apprentice was a young person, as young as 10 years old, who would learn at the master's side. Some examples of apprenticeships were for shoemakers, clockmakers, hatters, seamstresses, and even bakers.

The practice of apprenticeships began sometime during the Middle Ages. A young person would work and learn a trade beside a professional, and in return, receive food and lodging. It was usually a contract for seven years. Until then, the apprentice was an unpaid servant who received training in return for their work. Most apprentices continued to work in their trades, but not all of them were able to become successful enough to be masters or own their own shops.

Eventually, groups called **guilds** were formed in order to govern and control the quality of the product the masters and apprentices made. Guilds could be powerful. They even controlled the prices for which the craftsmen could sell their goods. As guilds began to grow and control more of the cottage industry, women were pushed out of work, and creativity and innovation suffered.

Besides apprenticeships, there were other ways of producing goods without machines. **Indentured servants**, who were especially common in America, agreed to work for an employer for a period of seven to eight years. In exchange, the employer provided money for immigration to his city or country, as well as food and shelter. In some cases, but not always, the servant also had the opportunity to learn a valuable skill. Thousands of early colonial Americans arrived as indentured servants. In many situations, it was nothing more than a form of slavery.

 During the 1600s, up to 65 percent of travelers crossing the Atlantic Ocean from Great Britain and Ireland were indentured servants.[1]

Slavery around the world also provided unpaid labor. The **Atlantic Slave Trade** flourished between the 16th and 19th centuries. Millions of Africans were forcibly removed from their continent and shipped under brutal conditions to England, Europe, and North and South America where they were put to work.

---

1. Newman, 2015

The end of the cottage industry

During the 1700s, people in Britain began to live a little longer. They had more children. A large population growth created a demand for the staples of life: growing families needed more food, cheaper clothes, and some kind of trade. This created a change in how people thought about living their lives. By the 1750s, new ideas and improvements, especially in **agriculture,** began to change how people worked. Inventors and scientists looked for ways to make life easier and solutions to get work done faster.

In the year 1733, **John Kay** invented a machine called the **flying shuttle**. John had grown up as the son of a wool manufacturer in Lancashire, England. He worked at his father's mill and recognized that the faster a man could weave, the more money he could make.

An old-fashioned loom. Photo courtesy of Shutterstock.com.

The flying shuttle was a type of **loom**, the frame-like device used to weave cloth. Looms held threads in one direction so other threads or material could be woven in from another direction. Before the flying shuttle, the weaver had to push the loom back in place when he arrived at the end, but with John Kay's invention, a simple pull on a cord would jerk it back into place at the beginning using a track.

The flying shuttle made weaving twice as fast, and manufacturers were happy to use it, but Kay did not receive any money for his invention and lost his fortune fighting for his rights in court. His invention, however, was the first step in creating machines that worked faster than people in the **textile**, or fabrics, industry.

FAST FACT The Spinning Jenny was a type of loom invented in 1764 by James Hargreaves. This weaver's frame had multiple spindles, or rods, to hold spools of wool or other material. A worker could do more, faster, and the invention was moved into manufacturing houses. It did not make very strong yarn, however, so as improvements were made, it lost its popularity.

By 1769, **Richard Arkwright** had invented the water frame — a spinning machine powered by water. Richard was also from Lancashire, but he began his career as a wig maker. Probably inspired by the **Spinning Jenny**, Richard's automatic machine was powered by water and worked better than its inspiration. He was successful with his invention; he found business partners, opened factories, and eventually operated with 5,000 workers.[2] He was knighted for his contributions in 1786, which earned him the title of "Sir Richard Arkwright."

In the year 1776, the same year the United States declared its independence from Great Britain, the Scottish inventor **James Watt** invented the steam engine. James was a mechanical engineer who originally wanted to

2. Britannica.com, 2017

make mathematical instruments. In 1712, he studied the invention of the **Newcomen steam engine** and realized it wasted too much energy. He improved the idea and patented the **Watt steam engine** in 1781. This engine was powerful enough to be used to run machines, mills, engines, and trains. It transformed the Industrial Revolution and the rest of the world.

The Watt steam engine did not just change transportation: it could be used with looms to weave cloth faster. Suddenly, one machine could take the place of several weavers. Savvy businessmen now just needed space to set up the machines and acquire a workforce to run them. Money from renters, business investments, inheritances, and the slave trade was used to set up buildings for these new machines.

Now, workers no longer worked at home. They traveled to their job to work beside others. The modern-day idea of factories was born, and the Industrial Revolution truly began.

The Revolution

The machines of the Industrial Revolution and its ideas spread through all of England and to other parts of the world. The giant inventions were expensive and took up a lot of space, so they were moved into factories where the workers who used them could be controlled. New and improved steam engines propelled some machines that took the place of labor once done by hand. They moved locomotives across the English and American countrysides at great speeds. Excited about the possibilities, America began exploring new inventions of its own.

Soon, men, women, and children who did not own or work on farms moved to cities to find jobs to support their families. This created problems like overcrowding, disease, and abuse. Critics worried that machines would someday replace all workers. This new world moved fast and was loud and dirty.

By the 1850s, most of the world had joined the revolution. It provided jobs, more readily available goods, and changed how people, especially women and children, were treated. However, countries like England and Russia gobbled up land and faraway territories to find more resources needed for the goods made inside of the factories. This created political problems and even led to wars.

Near the end of the Industrial Revolution in America, factories and businesses dotted the landscape of the northern United States. The slave trade in the American South had fueled industrial growth by contributing raw materials like cotton. Eventually, as the Age of the Machines began to slow its pace, a new revolution called for the freedom of every American, both inside and outside of the factories. The young country found itself in the middle of a civil war so that all men and women, no matter where they were born or the color of the skin, could be free to live and work where and how they wished.

Sparks In America

Slater the Traitor

In the beginning, the ideas and advancements of the Industrial Revolution took time catching fire in the heart of Americans. The people living "across the pond" from England weren't interested in fancy, expensive machines. There was too much land to work, and people were spread out. Early on, the idea of building a factory to hold machines and hundreds of workers didn't make a lot of sense.

One of the first sparks in America was lit by a man named Samuel Slater. Samuel was born in England, but after working in the cotton textile industry as a young man, he moved to America when he was about 21 years old. When he left, he had good knowledge of factory machines and wanted to use it. Because it was against British law to take any drawings of the machines, Samuel memorized the information he needed and found investors in Rhode Island to help him build similar machines and then the mills to operate them.

An image of Samuel Slater. Courtesy of the Public Domain.

An Early Industrial Woman

Samuel Slater married a creative, enterprising young woman named Hannah Wilkinson in 1791. Four years later, after working alongside her husband, Hannah invented the idea of a two-ply cotton sewing thread. This meant that instead of producing a single string, two strands of thread were wrapped around each other to form a single, thicker thread that was perfect for sewing. Hannah became the first American woman to receive a patent in 1793. She died shortly after in 1812, leaving behind six children.

In England, they called Samuel "Slater the Traitor" because he copied their machine ideas, but Samuel became very successful. He eventually owned more factories in Massachusetts and Connecticut.

Beginning with his first business in Rhode Island, Samuel created a system that worked in unity with the villages and families around the factories. Children as young as seven were hired for him to supervise. Later, entire families, and even women, came to work. The factory offered homes and education, which helped families and kept them close to work. This idea, called the **Rhode Island System**, eventually spread, and Samuel earned the nickname, "The Father of the American Factory System."

The cotton gin

A major invention for America would transform the ways things were done in the South and fuel major growth in the American economy as it stoked the fires of the new Industrial Revolution. The **Cotton Gin** — "gin" for engine — was a small, box-shaped machine that combed the small seeds out of raw cotton so that it did not have to be done by hand. It was invented by an educated farm boy who never gave up: **Eli Whitney**.

Eli was born in Massachusetts around 1765. His parents let him tinker around with tools as a boy, so by the time he was a young man, the neighbors knew they could ask him to fix their farm equipment. After saving money that he earned working as a mechanic, Eli went to college at Yale in Connecticut. He graduated in 1792 and found a job in South Carolina working as a tutor, but the plan fell through when he arrived, and he found himself homeless and unemployed with no relatives in the South to help him.

Fortunately for Eli, the widow of local war hero, Catharine Greene, let him stay at her large **plantation** house outside of Savannah, Georgia. One night, Eli listened to some of her friends complain about the labor and cost of separating cotton seeds, and it gave him a great idea. Once again, a strong woman stood up behind an early inventor, and Mrs. Greene encouraged Eli to invent the machine. He did, and then returned to the North to file a patent.

"Cotton grown by slaves in the American South fueled the Industrial Revolution."[3]

Unfortunately, the cotton gin, with its crank and combs that separated seeds, was so popular and successful, copies of it were made before Eli could legally claim the invention, and he never received any money for it. Eli did not die poor, though; he approached the American government a few years later and offered to manufacture 10,000 muskets, including **bayonets** and **ramrods**, with interchangeable parts. The government paid him an enormous amount of money for his new inventions, and he manufactured them at an **armory** in Hamden, Connecticut. Visitors can see the Eli Whitney museum there today.

A burning fire of industry and development

As the sparks of the early American Industrial Revolution grew into flames, the country began to grow, and people found that with hard work, the American dream was as possible as ever. Mills and factories spread, dotting what was once farmland. They attracted people to the towns, and the townships grew into bustling cities.

New businesses found they needed ways to borrow money to get started, so state governments set up credit systems to loan entrepreneurs the money

3. Frader, 2006

to start up their mills and manufacturing factories. This, in turn, created a need for better roads and bridges, which also provided jobs and helped communities grow. Railroads soon crisscrossed the nation, carrying workers, resources, and useful products ready for the market.

Did Women Work on the Railroads?

The transcontinental railroad linked the United States by connecting Omaha, Nebraska, to Sacramento, California. It was built by two railroad companies: the Central Pacific Railroad and the Union Pacific Railroad. One company began building in the East and the other in the West until they met in Promontory, Utah on May 10th, 1869. This enormous feat took seven years, and American and Chinese men deserve much credit for the accomplishment. However, many white women traveled and camped with their husbands to be near them while they worked, and some Chinese women worked on the railroad, too. As the tracks gobbled up more and more Native American territory, men and women of the Paiute and Shoshone tribes were forced to sign treaties and work on the railroad because their lands and buffalo were being destroyed. One historical record insists that the Shoshone women were stronger than the white or Chinese men and that they had better backs.[4]

Another one of the biggest achievements in transportation during this era was the building of the **Erie Canal**. This 363-mile waterway connects the Great Lakes to the Atlantic Ocean. It provided jobs for new immigrants and a resource for goods to make their way west faster than wagon because of the newly invented steamboat. People were no longer stuck in one region or another. They could travel, and it was much better than using horses.

All of this work and invention created a new social class. Just as society had adapted in Britain, an American middle class gained its footing between the wealthy and the very poor. Workers could organize and protest their

4. CPRR.net, 2009

pay. People could "strike" and refuse to work until their employers made things right. This empowered society in many ways. Families could now have time off to rest or to travel. It fueled even more time-saving inventions, like the sewing machine, that not only could be used in manufacturing, but could help women at home.

An old photograph of the Erie Canal. Courtesy of Shutterstock.com.

The American Civil War between 1861-1865 was a terrible time, but it did not halt advancements in science and medicine. The telegraph carried messages, and machine-operated printing presses produced newspapers. Oil that was discovered just before the Civil War was used as another energy resource, and the demand fueled the building of oil drilling and refining factories.

At the close of the 19th century, some Americans had electricity to light their homes. Along with roads, bridges, and railroads, telephone lines began to appear thanks to the discovery of Alexander Graham Bell. The first towering skyscraper was built in Chicago, and many Americans now had more power than ever in their lives with jobs, unions, and the right to vote.

During all of this change, one steady influence was pulled to and fro between the family home and the industrial workplace: women. Many women had found a world they had never known before. The early historical ideas of a quiet, submissive, woman working only around the house and garden began to change. Now, there were opportunities for women to think, learn, work, and contribute to a flowering society.

Mother Leaves Home

As the first seeds of the Industrial Revolution were planted, business owners realized the harsh conditions and low pay would not be tempting to many men unless they were desperate for work. Children were easy to come by and could be paid very little, but women, they realized, would be perfect.

Wealthy women did not have to work, but for the poor there was little choice. Children and young women were some of the first to be employed away from home at mills and other manufacturing factories. Females were seen as meek and obedient. They were easier to control, discipline, and would accept pay lower than men, because it had always been that way. Also, women and children usually had smaller hands, which worked well for moving safely in and around equipment. More and more families found that mothers had to leave home and work in order for the family to survive.

Frustrated with the demanding roles of women in the home and now in the workforce, one woman wrote: "…a young woman must toil incessantly at some handicraft from five years old and upwards, where and how is she to learn some needlework, cookery, economy, cleanliness, and all the 'arts of home?'"[5]

As the middle class grew, women eventually found that they had more career options. Some chose to pursue politics and social reform. Many took on the causes of children, struggling women, and the plight of factory workers slaving away in shameful conditions. But it would take time.

Shameful conditions

Just as in Great Britain, greedy employers in the early years of the Industrial Revolution took advantage of the relatively low respect society held for women and brought them to work with just enough pay to keep them — and under terrible conditions, at that.

Factories began operating in the early mornings. There was often little natural light and no fresh air. Toxic chemicals and materials were breathed in. Long hours and little food caused sickness, but workers had to come work even if they were sick, and that spread disease. Some factories would even lock their female workers inside. No one could leave without permission, and the only way in or out was by one approved door.

Men held most of the supervisory positions. In many instances, bells commanded when work began and ended and when one of the two or three breaks could be taken. No talking was allowed.

FAST FACT The smallest children who worked in the factories were called "scavengers." They had to climb underneath the dangerous machines while they were operating and pick up pieces of loose cotton or clean up oil.

---

5. Frader, 2006

If women and children did not die in accidents, they often passed way from illness caused by exhaustion or poor nutrition. Most factory workers during the early Industrial Revolution were diseased or handicapped by the time they were 40 years old. The large majority of children either died before they turned 16 or had physical deformities like missing fingers, twisted ankles, or knees that turned inward.

Politically Active Women

Grace Abbot was an early political activist who fought for the rights of children. She was born in Grand Island, Nebraska in 1878. Her family had supported the Underground Railroad system that protected runaway slaves before and during the Civil War and later fought for the right for women to vote. Grace worked for the Children's Bureau of the Department of Labor. She fought for the rights of small, working children under 16 years old to protect them from neglect and abuse.

In coal mines, both in America and Great Britain, small children were forced to move up and down narrow shafts and scramble through small, unsafe spaces. Some children, including girls, were tied to coal carts which they dragged through narrow tunnels on their hands and knees, often naked to endure the horrible heat.

One of the shameful realities of the Industrial Revolution is this treatment of women and children. Without the eventual outcry of caring men and women in powerful positions, as well as unions who protested the cruelty, things might have never changed.

Chapter Two

The Girls Of Lowell Mill

When people think about unions or workers' rights, they usually don't imagine young, tired women working like busy, tireless ants in a cotton mill. It is because of early working women in the mills during the Industrial Revolution that we have shorter work weeks and days. Because of their pioneering and brave efforts, we have workers' rights and **compensation** today**.**

A mill could be small enough to hold nothing more than a waterwheel and a grindstone that produced flours, or as America soon learned at the turn of the early 19th century, giant enough to store power-driven looms, weavers, and the workers to run them.

Not all Americans liked the idea of factories at first. Thomas Jefferson had helped sell the nation on the idea that farming — or the agricultural system — was the most important way to keep the country strong and thriving. He believed small, independent workers and businesses were best for democracy rather than large-scale companies who collected power and controlled people's wages and lives. **Jeffersonians** were against the idea of industrialization in America.

The famous American politician **Alexander Hamilton** felt differently. He embraced the possibilities offered by an industrial revolution. He pushed for the government to offer credit to help businessmen build mills and factories. To make industrialization sound better, the Federalist and Whig parties, who thought like Hamilton, focused on the possibilities of growth, wealth, and the trade that industrialization could provide.

A map of the Lowell Mills from 1850. Image courtesy of the Public Domain.

As mills were built in America, the **Boston Manufacturing Company** built the first major power-driven textile mill, the Lowell Mill, outside of Boston, Massachusetts in 1814. The area was named after the creator, Francis Cabot Lowell, who introduced the idea of a planned town built around the factory to integrate family life into a work life. The factories built around the mill in Lowell stretched the boundaries of what a workforce could do by setting in place rules about where to live and how to dress, behave, and socialize, both within its walls and within the surrounding community.

The Mill

The Lowell Mill company was more than just one building, but each created a product from start to finish under one roof. Among shafts and conveyor belts, workers with different jobs performed each step of the process.

There was something different about the workers at Lowell Mill, though. Instead of men and their families, the workers were all young women.

Within a few years of the mill being built, the new Erie Canal provided ways for young men to travel west in search of jobs with better pay than farming. Cheaper goods were also shipped in and out from the West, creating competition for businesses in the East and making it easier for low-income families to buy things they once couldn't afford.

In order for the factories at the mill to operate, workers had to be in place and ready to begin at the first bell of the day, no matter which job they were assigned. Supervisors started the machines and set the speed, and everyone would hurry to keep pace with the equipment, working together like bees in a hive.

The factories at Lowell Mill had rule books called handbooks. The rules from the 1848 handbook read:

> The overseers are to be always in their rooms at the starting of the mill, and not absent unnecessarily during working hours. They are to see that all those employed in their rooms, are in their places in due season, and keep a correct account of their time and work. They may grant leave of absence to those employed under them, when they have spare hands to supply their places, and not otherwise, except in cases of absolute necessity.[6]

Within 20 years of being built, Lowell Mill became quite the industrial village. Five different companies built cotton mills and offered good pay. The word soon got out that they would hire females, so widows, unmarried women, and young girls who needed to help their families or save them-

---

6. Avery, 1848

selves came by the hundreds. It gave women freedom and their own wages, but it came at a price. The newly hired young girls and women would soon find that like in England, the mills came with a dark side.

> All persons entering into the employment of the company, are considered as engaged for twelve months, and those who leave sooner, or do not comply with all these regulations, will not be entitled to a regular discharge. –Handbook to Lowell

The owners of the mills took advantage of the growing population of young women wanting to work. Eventually, critics began to complain that factory work, especially at Lowell Mill, was too harsh for women. They believed factory girls picked up bad behaviors, practiced poor morals and values, were uneducated, and that their health was in danger. Some pointed out that industrialization had no government limits or controls and that workers were forced to lives in another form of urban slavery.

> The company will not employ anyone who is habitually absent from public worship on the Sabbath, or known to be guilty of immorality.

> A physician will attend once in every month at the counting-room, to vaccinate all who may need it, free of expense.

> Anyone who shall take from the mills or the yard, any yarn, cloth or other article belonging to the company, will be considered guilty of stealing and be liable to prosecution.

> –Handbook to Lowell[7]

---

7. Avery, 1848

Factory Girls

By 1840, the mills employed up to 8,000 women. They called the women "operatives" because they operated the machines, and it sounded more professional. The truth was, these women came mostly from farming backgrounds; although some did have a little education, they weren't treated like professionals.

Factory work was still considered the least respectable job a woman could take outside the home. Although many worked to send brothers or other relatives to school or because they were in poverty, it represented a lack of purity and wholesomeness to others in higher society.

Factory girl Harriet Robinson grew up to be a popular and respected wife of a newspaper editor. She wrote about her experience working for Lowell Mill, saying that a factory girl was, "in the eyes of her overseer…a brute, a slave, to be beaten, pinched and pushed about."[8]

The first girls that worked for Lowell Mill came from upper New England, many from farms. As business spread and factories grew, immigrants later began to take their places. These young women came from Canada, Ireland, Poland, and Greece. They believed the stories that said the streets of New York were paved with gold. Imagine their surprise when they arrived and couldn't find work.

Altogether, because of the different cultures and beliefs, the mills became like a giant melting pot of flavors. Harriet Robinson described her co-workers in her writings:

---

8. Ibid

[T]he early factory girls were not all country girls. There were others also, who had been taught that "work is no disgrace." There were some who came to Lowell solely on account of the social or literary advantages to be found there. They lived in secluded parts of New England, where books were scarce, and there was no cultivated society. They had comfortable homes, and did not perhaps need the money they would earn; but they longed to see this new 'City of Spindles,' of which they had heard so much from their neighbors and friends, who had gone there to work...[9]

The immigrant workers settled into areas of the industrial village with people from their own home countries. They didn't mind the hard work; they were already used to it, and they needed a job. The girls went to church together and to parties and dances. They struggled with understanding how to be a part of two cultures, but by sticking together they made friendships and some found husbands.

The long work day

The factory girls at Lowell Mill worked between 12 to 14 hours a day. They did not get weekends off, but worked on Saturdays, too. Some began at six in the morning every day, and others started even earlier at five.

Most of the young women working at Lowell Mill were between 16 and 25 years old, but some were as young as 10. They called the smallest children, "**doffers**." Doff means to take off or remove, and the doffers took off the full bobbins of thread on the machines and replaced them with empty ones when they were full. This usually took place for about 15 minutes of every hour. Some supervisors would allow the small children to play outside, to

---

9. Robinson, 1898

read, or to knit when they weren't working, but they had to stay on duty for the 14-hour day.

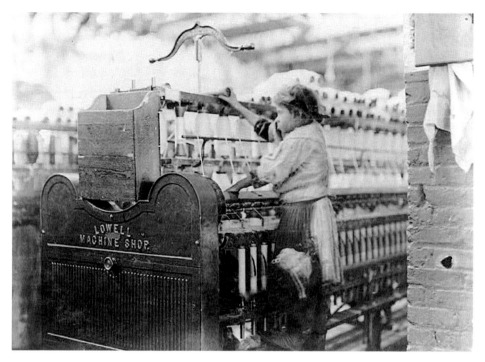

A photograph of a young girl working a machine in Lowell Mill.
Courtesy of the Public Domain.

 FAST FACT Doffers were paid about $2 a week for 84 hours of work.

Looms and weaving machines were so loud it was hard to talk or even think. Besides being deafening, the factory was oily and dusty. The companies kept the rooms hot and humid because it helped keep the thread from breaking. The workers felt like it was easier to work without air blowing things around, even though it made so many sick and tired.

The factory girls worked between eight and 10 months of the year. This meant a few months without pay, so some would return home or teach school during the summer to survive. It was a hard way of life, but it provided some independence to young women who didn't have any better options.

A room and a bed

Lowell Mill had to provide some place for all of its young women to live. Just as the Rhode Island System kept workers living around the factory in family homes, the mill offered long rows of boarding houses for the girls right next to work.

Older women, called **boarding keepers**, were paid by the company to watch over the workers. They were responsible for ensuring that the young factory women behaved, used good manners, and even went to church. If anyone caused a problem, the boarding keeper would report the rule-breaking to the mill supervisors. This could mean being fired and even being **blacklisted** from working at any other factories.

One 1846 historical record detailed how the girls lived outside of the factory:

> The young women sleep upon an average six in room; three beds to a room. There is no privacy, no retirement here; it is almost impossible to read or write alone, as the parlor is full and so many sleep in the same chamber. A young woman remarked to us, that if she had a letter to write, she did it on the head of a band-box, sitting on a trunk, as there was not space for a table. So live and toil the young

women of our country in the boarding-houses and manufactories, which the rich and influential of our land have built for them.[10]

Just like the mill had rules for working inside the factories, they made a rulebook for living in the boarding houses, too:

Boarding House Rules from the Handbook to Lowell, 1848

- The tenants of the boarding-houses are not to board, or permit any part of their houses to be occupied by any person, except those in the employ of the company, without special permission.

- They will be considered answerable for any improper conduct in their houses, and are not to permit their boarders to have company at unseasonable hours.

- The doors must be closed at ten o'clock in the evening, and no person admitted after that time, without some reasonable excuse.

- The keepers of the boarding-houses must give an account of the number, names and employment of their boarders, when required, and report the names of such as are guilty of any improper conduct, or are not in the as are guilty of any improper conduct, or are not in the regular habit of attending public worship.

- The buildings, and yards about them, must be kept clean and in good order; and if they are injured, other-wise than from ordinary use, all necessary repairs will be made, and charged to the occupant.

- The sidewalks, also, in front of the houses, must be kept clean, and free from snow, which must be removed from them immediately after it has ceased falling; if neglected, it will be removed by the company at the expense of the tenant.

---

10. Umbc.edu, n.d.

- It is desirable that the families of those who live in the houses, as well as the boarders, who have not had the kine pox, should be vaccinated, which will be done at the expense of the company, for such as wish it.

- Some suitable chamber in the house must be reserved, and appropriated for the use of the sick, so that others may not be under the necessity of sleeping in the same room.

JOHN AVERY, Agent.[11]

Life at Lowell Mill was hard. Still, some of the young women were used to other terrible conditions in their families or working on farms. They felt the freedom and the fellowship with other young women made it worthwhile. Other women were shocked at the rules and conditions and how they were treated. Critics told them they would be ruined and that few would ever marry, and sometimes they were right. Because the girls became sick or worn out over time, most workers didn't stay long before heading back to their families or hometowns.

Orestes A. Brownson was a Vermont activist and writer who felt strongly about the treatment of workers in factories. In an article for the Boston Quarterly Review, he wrote: "The poor girls when they can toil no longer go home to die. The average working life is about three years."[12]

A storm began to brew at Lowell Mill. Women wanted to work, but they wanted to be treated like human beings.

---

11. Ibid
12. Orestes, 1840

Women, Unite!

Lowell Mill formed its rules around the idea that young women needed guidance to be efficient and useful while remaining virtuous. For some, the rules were just too strict. With encouragement from those who spoke out, it wasn't long before the American ideals of freedom and individual rights seeped into the minds and hearts of the girls working in the factories.

Within 10 to 15 years of the mill's beginnings, the workers began to speak up and fight against the strict boarding houses, factory hours and rules, and the overall conditions required for a woman to work at the mill. Machines became bigger and faster, and the children and women were expected to keep up. It was too dangerous. To make matters worse, as American girls quit, the newly hired immigrants were paid less and expected to do more.

 Lucy Larcom is a famous schoolteacher and poetess who was sent to work in the factories in 1835 at just 11 years old. She began to write while working for Lowell Mill and became involved in a young women's literary magazine during her 10 years there. The mill girls soon were respected for being talented in literature and arts. Lucy saw both the good and the bad. Although she "hated the confinement, noise, and lint-filled air," she considered herself lucky to have a job and enjoyed the friendships she had there.[13]

The mill owners cut pay for the factory girls in 1834. Following the lead of some girls who led a two-day revolt at the Boston Manufacturing Company in 1821, the girls decided to protest, or **strike**, and refuse to work. The crowd of young women grew as they marched from building to building, inviting others to join them and sign a **petition** that said they wouldn't work unless their pay was returned back to the original wage. They published their own newspaper and demanded fair pay and shorter hours.

---

13. Howe, Walker Daniel

People were shocked at the display of stubbornness, even though the girls claimed their right as American workers. A newspaper in Boston reported the women's strike:

> The number soon increased to nearly 800. A procession was formed, and they marched about the town, to the amusement of a mob of idlers and boys, and we are sorry to add, not altogether to the credit of Yankee girls….We are told that one of the leaders mounted a stump and made a flaming Mary Wollstonecraft speech on the rights of women and the iniquities of the "monied aristocracy," which produced a powerful effect on her auditors, and they determined to "have their way if they died for it."[14]

The 1834 strike was short, lasting only one week. Supervisors soon rid themselves of the troublemakers, and the factories went back to operating at full power within no time. One angry manager complained that it was "an amizonian display" with "a spirit of evil."[15]

Two years after the first strike, the girls protested again and made sufficient noise to shut down the mill long enough to hurt business. They were defeated again, but this time around they learned from their mistakes: they needed to be better prepared and better organized.

Within 10 years they were ready. In 1844, even though women still did not have the right to vote in the United States, the women of the factories organized the official women's union in America at Lowell Mill. They named it the **Lowell Female Labor Reform Association (LFLRA)**, and it became successful at last, protecting the working women of Lowell Mill.

---

14. Robinson, 1898
15. Connectsemass.org, 1834

A photo of female factory workers in the early 20th century.
Courtesy of The Kheel Center for Labor-Management Documentation
and Archives, Cornell University Library

One of the first things the LFLRA did was demand a shorter workday with a legal cap. It sent petitions around the state of Massachusetts asking for people to sign their demand for the state legislature to agree to a 10-hour workday at Lowell Mill. Within two years, they had over 5,000 signatures. The association published newsletters, organized groups at mills in other towns and states, and went head-to-head with the Massachusetts politicians who opposed them.

FAST FACT Sarah Bagley of New Hampshire became the first president of the Lowell Female Labor Reform Association. She fought for better work hours and pay then later went on to become a political activist for women's rights.

The union eventually won the right to a 10-hour workday at Lowell Mill. Not long after, New Hampshire passed a 10-hour workday law for the entire state. The factory girls of Lowell Mill had grown up to become strong and powerful women who recognized their right to be treated as equals to men in society. They were still years away from achieving true equal rights, but they had learned to come together and fight for justice, and in their own ways, planted the seeds of women's rights decades before the fight for **women's suffrage**.

A Factory Girl Writes Home

Mary Paul was a factory girl who started working at Lowell Mill in 1845. She wrote many letters home to her father about life at the mills, many of which have been preserved by the Vermont Historical Society. Even with petitions and protests, life could be dangerous working in the factories.

Lowell Dec 21st, 1845

Dear Father

I received your letter on Thursday the 14th with much pleasure. I am well which is one comfort. My life and health are spared while others are cut off. Last Thursday one girl fell down and broke her neck which caused instant death. She was going in or coming out of the mill and slipped down it being very icy. The same day a man was killed by the [railroad] cars. Another had nearly all of his ribs broken. Another was nearly killed by falling down and having a bale of cotton fall on him.[16]

When the Civil War began in 1861, Lowell Mill sold off its cotton and supplies to make fast cash. The business never fully recovered from the long war, and by the turn of the century, it was too old-fashioned to compete with new factories and industries. Though still producing, many businesses running the mill felt it was time to close or leave by World War I. By the 1950s, very little trace of what was once a thriving social experiment during

16. Aflcio.org, n.d.

the Industrial Revolution remained. During the 1960s, a museum and historic park were planned to revitalize the area that had almost disappeared.

The girls of Lowell Mill made their mark on American history. They left behind a legacy for future American women who wished to organize or be represented by workforce unions. Today, these unions protect teachers, police women, pilots, and others in the workplace so that they are treated equally and fairly in whatever career they may choose.

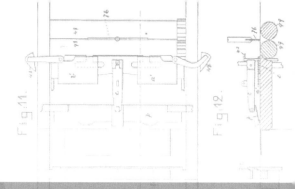

Chapter Three

Mattie At The Mill

The Industrial Revolution not only became an opportunity for women to work, but for women to invent and claim their own rights to their ideas, even though they could not own property or vote. Margaret Knight, or Mattie, as she was sometimes called, was born in 1838 at the height of glory for the cotton mills spinning away in Massachusetts. The new machine age was her world, and it affected her life.

Living far up north in York, Maine, her family probably had no idea that the little girl who preferred playing with tools instead of dolls would be one of the first recognized and successful female inventors in American history. The funny thing is, it wasn't because of hammers or nails. It all started with paper.

FAST FACT One of the earliest mentions of paper comes from Marco Polo. A Chinese man named Ts'ai Lun invented paper in China in 105 A.D. Polo wrote that the Chinese made paper from vegetable fibers but guarded how they produced it to keep it secret.[17]

---

17. de Safita, 2002

Throughout the ages, people had carried items in whatever resources were available. They used clay pots, baskets made from reeds, bags made from animal bladders, pouches of leather, jute sacks, and barrels and trunks made from wood. Paper was used for keeping records or writing books and letters.

Paper was expensive, but at the dawn of the Industrial Revolution in France, a man name Louis-Nicolas Robert invented a machine that would make rolls, instead of sheet, of paper. The idea was a success from Europe to Great Britain and across the sea to America, and paper soon became available to everyone.

With more paper around, people realized it could be folded and used for more things than bills or love letters. Paper could be used to wrap presents or fragile gifts. Shop owners realized they could package small amounts of goods for customers to take home. The idea of a bag tried to take shape, but it took a long time to fold them and glue them together, and it didn't always work.

Ingenious inventors tried to come up with ways to make bags out of paper. One man, Francis Wolle of Pennslyvannia, applied for a patent to make the first paper bag machine. The invention used steam with glue and made bags shaped like flat envelopes. It was a success for a while, but it was hard to carry big packages that were long and wide and did not always stay together.

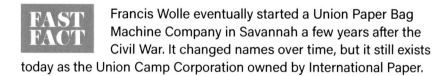 Francis Wolle eventually started a Union Paper Bag Machine Company in Savannah a few years after the Civil War. It changed names over time, but it still exists today as the Union Camp Corporation owned by International Paper.

The little girl named Mattie would change that and put her stamp on every day American life by inventing the paper bags we use today.

Even as a little girl, Margaret Knight knew she was different from other children because of her curious, creative mind. Her family left Maine and moved to New Hampshire when she was small. She grew up poor and did not have the opportunity to get much of an education, but she made the best out of it by making toys like sleds and kites for her brothers and sisters.

> As a child, I never cared for things that girls usually do; dolls never possessed any charms for me. I couldn't see the sense of coddling bits of porcelain with senseless faces: the only things I wanted were a jack-knife, a gimlet, and pieces of wood. My friends were horrified. I was called a tomboy; but that made very little impression on me. I sighed sometimes, because I was not like the other girls; but wisely concluded that I couldn't help it, and sought further consolation from my tools. I was always making things for my brothers; did they want anything in the line of playthings, they always said: "Mattie will make them for us." I was famous for my kites; and my sleds were the envy and admiration of all the boys in town.[18]

Life for the Knight family became worse after Margaret's father died when she was only 12 years old. Everyone had to go to work, even the girls. For Margaret, that meant the cotton mills.

At least one of Margaret's brothers who worked at the mills was an overseer, and this not only gave her a job, but the opportunity to see how the factory — and its equipment — operated. One day, she saw an accident happen right before her eyes. A shuttle, the frame that rested on the loom, came flying off when it hit a snagged thread, and its steel tips stabbed a nearby worker, reportedly a young boy.

---

18. Hanaford, 2011

The inventor in Margaret went right to work, and the young teenager invented a gadget that would stop the machine's motion if something became caught in it or got in its way. She was not even 13 years old yet, but the invention worked and made the looms at the mill safer. Soon the idea spread from one factory to another, and before long, everyone in the textile industry used the stopping device.

Even with her gifted mind, work was grueling at the mills. Margaret did not know about laws and patents when it came to the rights of inventors, but she knew her invention was being used by everyone to make life safer.

 A daguerreotype was a type of photographic image that used an iodine-sensitized silvered plate and mercury vapor.

She didn't earn any money for her first device, but she quickly understood that she could make some with her clever, useful ideas. A few years later, Margaret quit her job as a factory girl and learned other trades, like working with upholstery, which covers furniture, and making **daguerreotypes**, a type of early photograph. Armed with more knowledge and ideas, when the job opportunity came to move to Massachusetts and work for the **Columbia Paper Bag Company**, she decided to leave her family behind and took it.

The Folding Bag Machine

The Columbia Paper Bag Company in Springfield hired workers, including women, to make the flat, envelope-style bags used for carrying goods. Margaret was a single woman, but her continued education learning things like home repair and engraving made her a perfect fit for the job.

When she began to work for the company, she found herself surprised at the lack of innovation and creativity. The process for making the paper bags by hand was slow and clumsy. She immediately went home and wrote in her journal: "I am told that there is no such machine known as a square-bottomed machine. I mean to try away at it until I get my ideas worked out."[19]

The idea of a flat-bottomed bag was left to artisans and craftsmen because it was time consuming and fancy. Not many people had considered the idea of making an automatic paper bag folding machine for bags that could stand upright.

Margaret was different. She had already improved safety at the mills. She had also learned about patents and laws for claiming ownership of new inventions. Without telling her bosses at work, the independent young woman stubbornly sketched machine ideas in her free time, inventions that might work well enough to cut, fold, and glue a paper bag together just by turning a crank.

After six months, Margaret had a working model made of wood. It was wobbly, but it got the job done. The machine had a "guide finger and plate-knife holder" that attached to machines like the ones the factory already used. Margaret was able to make more than 1,000 paper bags with it!

Because she had studied about patents, Margaret knew that in order be granted one for her idea, she would have to make the machine again out of iron and prove that it worked. She took her wooden model to a local machine shop in Boston and asked the machinist to copy her design. It worked, but it needed some improvements. She decided to take it to someone else, and that is when her idea was stolen.

---

19. Meares, 2016

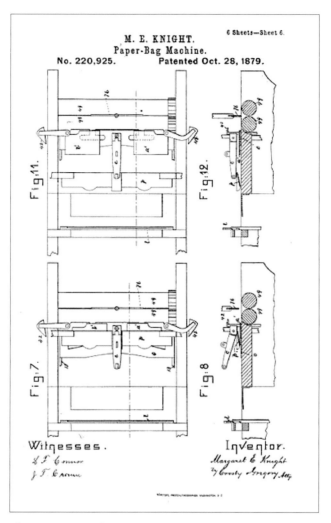

The 1879 patent for Margaret Knight's Paper-Bag Machine.
Image courtesy of the Public Domain.

FAST FACT The America Package Museum is an online exhibition website that features images of packages designed during the early 20th Century.[20] Visitors can view pictures of containers for food, drinks, medicine, and household products like gum, oatmeal, Band-Aid, Coca Cola, or shampoo.

20. Packagemuseum.com, n.d.

At the second machine shop, Margaret watched over the process and allowed a visiting machinist to watch the new model, or **prototype**, being built. The man's name was **Charles F. Annan**. Annan wanted to be an inventor, too, and he didn't appear to care how he received credit or the money for his ideas. With the iron prototype working, Margaret applied for her first patent, but it was rejected. Charles Annan had already sent in an application to patent her design and had recieved it, so Margaret was denied.

Margaret was about 33 years old at the time. She was single and didn't have a great deal of money stashed away, but the determined lady gathered up all of her income and savings and hired a lawyer for $100. She was going to sue.

Margaret took Annan to court. She filed a lawsuit for "patent interference" and provided the court with 16 days' worth of witnesses and testimonies. Along with help from those who helped her build the prototype, she had notes in her journals and drawings of her idea from beginning to end. The machinists at the second shop testified that Annan had come to visit and watched the machine being built and tested.

FAST FACT The United States Patent and Trademark Office, located in Alexandria, Virginia, is the government organization that grants patents and trademarks. Its purpose is to promote science and the "useful arts" for authors and inventors. Visitors to the office's website, https://www.uspto.gov/, can search for an existing patent or learn how to apply for a new one.

Annan had no serious proof that he had invented the new paper bag machine. He argued that he'd made changes to make the idea he saw in the shop better. He insisted his machine was different, although he could not tell the court how he first came up with the idea. The man went even further to insult Margaret's claim to the invention by saying women were not smart enough to understand how machines worked because machinery and manufacturing were complicated processes.

The courts decided in Margaret's favor, proving Annan to be a dishonest fraud. Margaret was awarded the patent on October 28, 1879. She was offered $50,000 for the rights to her patent, but she courageously refused. Instead, she found a business partner and created the **Eastern Paper Bag Company**.

Margaret's paper bag machine spread around the world. The amazing invention could take the place of 30 workers and produce a high number of bags at a much faster rate. The Queen of England, Queen Victoria, awarded her the **Royal Legion of Honor**.

Today, a working model of Margaret's invention is held at the **National Museum of American History** in Washington, D.C. It is proof that women have always had the ability to create, invent, and produce when allowed to live fully up to their potential. Margaret Knight's courage and determination to succeed in science and engineering at a time when very few women held patents pushed the growing boundaries of the Industrial Revolution in American society, and, most importantly, forward into the hearts and minds of women.

Patents, Plaques, And Bragging Rights

Margaret didn't waste any time after she started her own paper bag company. There were too many problems waiting in the world of manufacturing that needed her creative touch. She continued to invent while living in Massachusetts. She bought a workshop in Boston and became an associate of the **Knight-Davidson Motor Company** after inventing a **sleeve valve engine**.

Now that she had the hang of how to apply and win patents, Margaret turned some of her other ideas into inventions. She made a paper-feeding machine, a numbering machine, a machine that cut out the bottoms of shoes, a special reel for sewing machines, a robe clasp, dress and skirt shields, window frame parts, and even a barbecue spit for grilling meat.

Overall, Margaret applied for and was granted between 25 and 27 patents. She never married but lived alone, working on her devices between 1894 and 1914. It didn't make her rich. When she became sick in 1914, her net worth was less than $300, but she still was known to work up to 20 hours a day. Before she finished what the New York Times reported would be her 89th invention, she developed pneumonia and eventually died on October 12th of 1914. She was 70 years old.

Margaret Knight's inventions went on to serve both the industrial and home industries. She is remembered today as being one of the leading inventors of her time, who went from working as a factory girl during the Industrial Revolution to the female Thomas Edison of the early 20th century.

Chapter Four

Poor Little Rich Girl

Once there was a little girl called Hetty, who had so much money, she decided to save it and just make more. The richer she became, the more she tried to spend as little as possible. The people who knew her thought she was odd and stingy. The most successful businessmen in the country were afraid of her. Society called her "The Witch of Wallstreet," and she became one of the richest women in American history.

The Industrial Revolution made many families rich. Investors in oil, railroads, and trade made fortunes. The results of industrialization created a society of the very wealthy who lived like royalty and who went on to develop a new era in American History called the **Gilded Age.**

One of the first people to become wealthy during Industrial Revolution was a Frenchman named Eleuthere Irenee, or E.I. du Pont. He started a gunpowder mill in 1802. It supplied the United States government with the powder they needed for explosives to clear land for railroads and canals. du Pont turned his gunpowder company into a chemical company called DuPont, which is still a successful American company today.

The DuPont company invented nylon, Teflon, and the bulletproof material called Kevlar that policemen and women wear to protect themselves.

The famous Rockefeller family of New York became wealthy thanks to their ancestor John D. Rockefeller, who started an oil company and made his fortune around 1858. Rockefeller is considered America's first billionaire.

Because of the machinery and railroads, other famous families like the Vanderbilts and the Carnegies became some of the richest and most powerful families during the 19th century. But not all of the wealthy in American history were men…

Henrietta Howland Robinson was born in the whaling city of New Bedford, Massachusetts in 1834. At the time she was born, the factories at Lowell Mill were spinning away, but the Robinson family lived on the coast and that meant supporting themselves by fishing and participating in the sea trade.

Hetty

Henrietta was often called Hetty. Her father, Edward Robinson, married her mother, Abby Howland, and since Abby was the daughter of the most successful whaling family in the city, Edward inherited his wife's money and family trade.

The Howland family were Quakers, a peaceful, conservative religious group who worked hard and lived lives based on high moral values. This meant Hetty was taught to be frugal and industrious. She grew up around her wealthy merchant grandfather, Gideon Howland, and was close to her father, too, since her mother was usually sick and too weak to spend time with her. This meant money was the language of love in her life, and she was taught to make it and save it.

The men in Hetty's life must have realized she was smarter than most other children her age. By the time she was 6 years old, she could read the newspaper and understand the financial section. She opened a bank account when she was only 8 years old. By the time she turned 13 years old, she was appointed to be the family bookkeeper, which meant she kept up with the family finances, including how they much they made and how much they spent. It was quite an unusual responsibility for a young girl born during the Industrial Revolution. Hetty read stock market reports and handled large sums of money.

Hetty was finally sent to school at age 16, and she studied at the Eliza Wing School in Sandwich, Massachusetts, the oldest town on Cape Cod. She later went on to study at a private school in Boston until she was 19 years old.

 According to Forbes[21] magazine, the top 10 richest families in America had their beginnings between 1802 and 1873, a clear result of the Industrial Revolution:

- 1802: Du Pont family, $14.5 billion

- 1841: Mellon family, $11.5 billion

- 1858: Rockefeller family, $11 billion

- 1864: Donnelley family, $1.6 billion

- 1865: Cargill /MacMillan family, $45 billion

- 1865: Milliken family, $4.4 billion

- 1865: De Young family, $2.5 billion

- 1870: Brown family, $12.8 billion

- 1873: Coors family, $4 billion

21. Savchuk, 2015

• 1873: Haas family, $3.7 billion

Hetty was just as unusual as a teenager as she was a little girl. She spent a great deal of time at the docks because of the family whaling business. Without a mother's influence, she picked up colorful language and did not spend any extra time on her appearance. Her aunt, Sylvia Howland, insisted she go to manners school and learn to dance, but even after finishing, she chose to follow in her grandfather's footsteps, making money and pinching every penny possible. When her father gave her over $1,000 for her entry into New York society around 1850, Hetty only spent $200 of it on a few satin gowns and a few pairs of gloves. Everything else, down to her underpants, was faded, old, and well-used.

At first, the wealthy citizens of New York society seemed to welcome and adore Hetty. She was described as a dark-haired "belle" with ringlets and a wonderful sense of humor. Many rich young men looking for an even richer wife knew Hetty would inherit her grandfather's money. They wasted no time trying to romance her, and even Great Britain's Prince of Wales asked her to dance twice at a ball after they met. She left him enchanted.

During the 1860s, when Hetty was well into her 30s, she met Edward Henry Green. Edward was born in Vermont in 1821 with wealth that allowed him to receive an education and travel. He spent time in Hong Kong and the Philippines before returning to New York as a silk merchant with $1 million in his pockets. Edward soon won Hetty over, and they had an extravagant wedding. According to the newspapers, it was a "grand and splendid social function."[22]

Hetty did not skip blindly into marriage. At a time when women had few rights or opportunities, she requested that Edward sign away his power to

---

22. *Boston Post*, 1902

access her money and agree that she would never be responsible for any of his debts. After the wedding, the couple moved to Manhattan to live in his home until circumstances carried them to London for a time. Meanwhile, Hetty looked for ways to make her own bank account grow.

> MARRIAGE OF A RICH SPINSTER.—
> Hetty H. Robinson, with many millions in her own right, and the claimant of two more millions in the famous "Howland will case," at New Bedford, Mass., was married at the residence of Henry Grinnell, New York city, July 11, to Edward H. Green, of the house of Russell & Sturgis. It will be remembered that Hetty claims to break her aunt Howland's will on the ground of a prior contract between herself and aunt, that neither should marry, and that the survivor should be sole heir to the other. The course of popular opinion and law having gone rather hard with Hetty, the aged spinster has evidently concluded to take unto herself a husband and have done with it.

A newspaper clipping of Hetty and Edward Green's marriage announcement. Image courtesy of Semi-Weekly Wisconsin, 24 Jul 1867, Newspapers.com

Hetty The Investor

Hetty Howland Robinson, now Hetty Green, was already rich before she decided to marry. Her mother, who was never in good health, died in 1860, when Hetty was about 25. Abby Robinson left her daughter an inheritance worth $8,000.

Hetty's father, Edward, didn't believe she needed that kind of money. He stopped her from receiving any of the inheritance from her mother until his own death. Ever frugal and even somewhat paranoid, he told Hetty that people would come after her and the family money, even if they had to kill her. Before he passed away, five years after his wife, he told Hetty he had been poisoned.

After his death, Edward Robinson finally gave Hetty the entire family fortune of $5 million and a trust fund, but required that one of his **executors**, or money managers, manage her. After all she had done for him, Hetty felt insulted and tried to bribe the executor. It didn't work out.

Aunt Sylvia, who had sent Hetty to school, promised her another fortune worth $20,000 when she died. That was a great deal of money to receive from a relative. In today's market, Aunt Sylvia's inheritance would be worth over half a million dollars.

 The Robinson estate at the time of Hetty's father's death would equal almost $80 million in today's currency.

When her father and aunt died, Hetty was still a young woman, and she was filthy rich.

One of the first acts of courage and defiance Hetty committed with her funds was to go to court. After her Aunt Sylvia died in 1865, the money she had promised to leave Hetty was left to charity in a new will. Hetty challenged the new will in a case labeled Robinson v. Mandell.

In court, Hetty showed a copy of the first will where her aunt promised to leave the money to her niece. Part of the will had a clause, or statement, that insisted any new wills would not be legal. After the court ruled the clause to be faked, Hetty was accused of **forgery** and lost the case. She fought for her aunt's money for five more years and finally was awarded a portion of it.

Because of the court case, Hetty Green was seen as ambitious, dangerous, and even greedy, but she felt it was only right to receive the money her aunt had promised her. People knew she had experience, millions of dollars, and had made sure her new marriage would not interfere with her income.

A relative from Baltimore who knew Hetty explained that it was just the Howland family way: "We're very, very independent people who go our own way, and that was the way Hetty was, too."[23]

Civil War bonds were pieces of paper that the government sold to raise money for the war. The bond could be bought back from the buyer after the war at a higher price. War bonds were used up through World War II. They were considered investments, sometimes risky, but a way for people to be patriotic and help fund the military to win the war.

Going to court to fight for her aunt's inheritance caused more problems for Hetty and her new husband. A few family cousins accused Hetty of forging her aunt's will and tried to have her charged with a crime. The couple packed their bags and moved to London to live in a hotel. There, Edward found work managing a few banks, and Hetty invested some of her money on new dollars being printed in the United States after the Civil War.

The investment in fresh American "greenbacks" was a success. Hetty made over $1 million investing in the recovering U.S. economy back home, and she took the rewards and sank them into the railroad industry. She made enormous amounts of money in the risk and learned a valuable lesson. For most of her career, Hetty would invest modest amounts of her fortune she could afford to lose and focus on investing it in valuable needs and services when the economy was shaky or others were too afraid to do it.

---

23. Laneri, 2018

Children and Collapse

The wealthy woman of the Howland and Robinson empire was not just a clever and thrifty investor living in London, she was a mother, too. Her first child, Ned, was born a year after her marriage in August of 1868, and a daughter, Sylvia, was born three years later in England. With the scandal of the lawsuit over her aunt's estate fading in the memories of Americans, the young family moved back to the United States.

Hetty Green's residence in Bellows Falls, Vermont.
Photograph courtesy of the Library of Congress.

Hetty had such a powerful reputation as a businesswoman and investor that people were disappointed when they first saw her. She didn't dress fancy or even bother to wear a corset at times. There were no parties or grand balls. The Greens lived very well, but they did not spread their money around or show off, and that made Hetty unpopular. Even the men of Wall Street who flocked to New York to see her when she came into town to open an account were not swept off their feet by her appearance or personality. Hetty was all business from her head down to her toes.

The wealthy Green family arrived in New England and settled in Bellows Falls, Vermont. Hetty didn't take it any easier on the Green family than she did on her own relatives. She reportedly fought with her husband's family and servants, and terrorized other businessmen in town.

About 20 years into their rocky marriage, one of Hetty's biggest investments fell apart, and her husband was partly to blame. The **John J. Cisco & Son** financial company had secretly loaned money to Edward, who could not pay back the debt, and they had used Hetty's investment money to back it up. After the company failed, and Hetty realized she'd lost $700,000 because of her own husband, she withdrew all of her investments from the business and kicked Edward out of the house.

After the financial disaster, Hetty paid her bills and took her money and deposited it with Chemical Bank. She next took her investing skills and fearlessness to Wall Street and conquered the market. Edward died in 1902, making her a widow. Dressing in plain, black clothes, avoiding publicity, and using a steely glare as she stalked the city streets, little Hetty from the whaling docks became known as the "Witch of Wallstreet."

 Hetty Green is recognized as a pioneer in the principle of value investing. This type of financing buys up stocks that the market has valued too low and that will likely increase a great deal in the future.

Hetty invested in real estate, scooped up late **mortgages,** and bought out failing businesses. She took advantage of others' bad luck, like buying ruined properties after fires swept through the city of Chicago and the great San Francisco earthquake. When Wall Street panicked, Hetty bought shares of stock cheap and held onto them until calm was restored and then sold high. By the time her grown children married, she was living in one apartment or another between New York and New Jersey and had earned the title of the Richest Woman in the World.

The World's Greatest Miser?

By the time Hetty ruled Wall Street, she had become a legend, not only for her investing gifts, but for her penny-pinching. Gossip spread that her son had a bad leg amputated after breaking it as a child because she had been unwilling to pay a skilled doctor. She'd opted instead for a clinic that offered free care for the poor. As an adult, Ned moved out of state and managed the family's properties in Chicago and Texas.

Sylvia, Hetty's daughter, did not marry until she was over 30 years old. Instead, she lived with her mother, who chased away all of her suitors. Convinced that anyone who liked her daughter just wanted money, Hetty did not approve any engagements until Sylvia met Matthew Astor Wilks, the great-grandson of John Jacob Astor.

John Jacob Astor was a famous businessman and investor who was successful during the early Industrial Revolution. He was so successful that he became the first multi-millionaire in America. Sylvia was allowed to marry Matthew in 1909 after he signed an agreement that surrendered any rights to her inheritance.

Separated from her husband and no longer living with her children, Hetty moved around from apartment to apartment to avoid paying taxes. Rumors that she was ridiculously tight-fisted with her money continued to spread. Landlords claimed she never heated the apartments or used hot water.

Some said Hetty would not eat anything more expensive than a 15-cent meat pie; others insisted she only ate cold oatmeal unless it could be heated up on a warm radiator. Her hired servants claimed she only had one dress and a set of underwear, and only allowed the dirty parts to be washed to save money on laundry detergent.

A sketch of Hetty Green in 1895, potentially at a 'referee's session' to dispute the accountings of the executor of her father's will concerning Mr. Robinson's estate. Courtesy of Shutterstock.com.

Hetty had no interest in renting out office space, either. The Witch of Wall Street conducted business in an office at the Seaboard National Bank of New York. She traveled back and forth to the bank with her paperwork in trunks, investing, lending, and buying with her money to watch it grow into the hundreds of millions. She traveled alone when necessary, sometimes over hundreds of miles, to collect debts, and bailed out the city of New York to keep the city running during the **Panic of 1907**.

Later life

As Hetty grew old and feeble, she had several **strokes,** a blocked artery or bleeding blood vessel in the brain. She developed a large **hernia**, or protruding part of an organ that's pushed through the body cavity. She refused the $150 surgery. Eventually, Hetty had to use a wheelchair and began to have paranoid thoughts that someone was trying to kidnap her.

By 1916, with her health seriously failing, Hetty moved in with her son, who had returned to New York to care for his mother. The 81-year-old financial genius died on July 3rd after, legend has it, arguing over skimmed milk. She left more than half of her fortune to churches, hospitals, and schools.

 Hetty Green's fortune was worth nearly $200 million in 1916; that would be over $2 billion in today's money.

Ned and Sylvia had their mother buried next to their father in Bellow Falls, Vermont. They took their inheritances and continued to invest like their mother had taught them, enjoying their fortunes and using it wisely. Ned left his money to his sister when he died in 1948, and Sylvia donated it to science and exploration projects at the Massachusetts Institute of Technology (MIT). She passed away three years later with a fortune nearly as valuable as her mother's, at about $2 million.

The legacy

Hetty Green was a legend in her own time. At the turn of the century, her name was even used in slang to reference wealth. In one short story by O. Henry, the American author of "The Skylight Room,"a character who looks wealthy but is not exclaims, "I'm not Hetty if I do look green. I'm just a poor little working girl."[24]

Her handwriting was messy, but her ways were not. Before she saved the day for New York during the 1907 Panic (one of three times she financed the city), she was reportedly seen going in and out of the home of famous banker John P. Morgan, along with Rockefeller and other millionaire businessmen. They were to meet at the request of the President of the United States, Theodore Roosevelt, and save the city.

Hetty always considered a debt an investment and charged **interest**, but she was honest and fair. Leading companies sent their owners and managers to beg for cash. She would help — at a price. Convinced she was nothing like some tycoons who took advantage of their workers or broke promises to banks and the government, she donated to charities, loaned money on low interest to churches, and sued companies she felt were dishonest to protect others — especially women. It is widely believed that she supplied the yearly income for several families out of personal generosity.

Was she really a witch? Hetty Green was born into money and education, influenced by strong, open-minded men of the age, and devout in her early Quaker beliefs. It is true that she wore black and had a stern outlook on life, but there was more behind the tattered black veil than many under-

---

24. O. Henry, 1906

stood. She once told a reporter, "My early training disciplined me towards pomp and show… My family has been wealthy for five generations. We need make no display to insure recognition of our position."[25] Yet, she is remembered today as the woman who inherited a fortune from the Industrial Revolution and became the first to rule Wall Street.

25. Sack, 2011

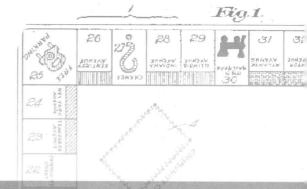

Chapter Five

The Woman Behind Monopoly

The Industrial Revolution may have created a new middle class, but it also made the rich richer. Life, and especially business, wasn't easy, and in the opinions of every day people like the Magies of Macomb, Illinois, the wealthy on Wall Street did not play fair. Sometimes it all seemed like a greedy game. Is it any wonder that Monopoly, the most popular U.S. board game of all time, was created during this period?

The original inventor of the game was lost for almost a century until a patent was discovered in 1973. Debates continue, but there is no denying that today's famous **Parker Brothers**' game was once the brainchild and creation of a colorful woman who was almost lost to history.

Little Lizzie

Education and opportunities continued to blossom for women at the turn of the century, but they had to be smarter, work harder, and stand up to critics with gritty determination. This meant they needed strong teachers to inspire them, and sometimes their best role models were their parents.

In the years leading up to the Civil War, a man name James Magie traveled with Abraham Lincoln and famous journalists across the state of Illinois debating slavery, territorial rights, and other issues that were dividing the country. James was a newspaper publisher and an **abolitionist** who supported the beliefs of Henry George.

 Henry George was an economist and author of a book called "Progress and Poverty." He believed people had the right to own anything they created, and that everything in nature belonged to all. He also proposed a single tax that would tax only land value and remove taxation on everything else. Besides writing, he was a talented, opinionated speaker. George's book inspired James Magie and his family. It would be a part of the inspiration for a new board game that would eventually be called Monopoly.

Just one year after President Lincoln was assassinated, a daughter was born to James and his wife, Mary Magie. They named her Elizabeth.

Elizabeth J. Magie did not have many siblings, so that may have played a part in her educational childhood that exposed her to journalism and politics. Her father owned part of the Canton Register newspaper, worked as a clerk in the Illinois state legislature, and ran for political office. The little girl, who liked to be called Lizzie, was encouraged to think, create, and to speak up for herself.

"I have often been called a 'chip off the old block', which I consider quite a compliment, for I am proud of my father for being the kind of an 'old block' that he is," said Elizabeth Magie.[26]

As Lizzie grew up, she had a strong belief in women's rights. Perhaps choosing a career over marriage was natural, but regardless, Lizzie decided to become a **stenographer** and work for the **Dead Letter Office**. Typewriters were new machines, considered confusing and strange by many. Typing out

---

26. Pilon, 2015

words instead of writing them was once a job for men, but because of the loss of men during the Civil War, jobs for men and women were changing.

 A stenographer types out words written in shorthand or spoken words in official meetings such as court.

Being a career woman and earning only $10.00 a week wasn't enough for Lizzie. She saw a need for typewriters to reel in paper without becoming wrinkled or jammed, so she invented a machine for it in 1893 when she was 26 years old. She was granted the patent for her gadget, a rare event for women before 1900. She also turned her attention to literature and the stage.

Between 1893 and 1895, Lizzie published a book of poems entitled "My Betrothed." Most of the poems were about romance and nature and had some very shocking lines. She also sold a story called "For the Benefit of the Poor" to a famous magazine, Frank Leslie's Popular Monthly. Her story was about a boy trying to sell candy in a theater to support his mother. The theme was one that she would use all of her life: Why do the rich get richer and the poor get poorer?

On stage, Lizzie liked to be funny. She was an actress while living in Washington and earned good reviews for her personality and presence. Audiences were known to burst into laugher when she wanted them to. She did not mind the attention, especially if she had a message to deliver.

Determined to make a name for herself and bring awareness to the struggles of womankind, Lizzie bought a newspaper ad and offered herself for sale. Calling herself a "young woman American slave," she wrote that she wasn't beautiful, but had character, strength, faith, and was "a born entertainer."[27]

---

27. Pilon, 2015

The shocking advertisement spread to other newspapers and magazines, and some people tried to shame her for the publicity stunt. Lizzie stood up to them, explaining that she was trying to let the world know that women were not like the machines of America's Industrial Revolution. "Girls have minds, desires, hopes and ambition."[28] In a way, the advertisement worked out for Lizzie. She was offered a job as a reporter and accepted it in 1906.

The 1900 census shows that Lizzie was independent and the head of her own household at 34 years old. Ten years later, she would finally settle down with a man 10 years older than herself named Albert Phillips. For someone who acted suspicious of marriage, Lizzie married happily and continued her work. She remained independent; she saved up and bought a home with land in Washington, D.C.

Years before her marriage, one of Lizzie's ongoing projects was a game for children. It was based on the books and speeches of the economist Henry George, whom her father had admired and supported. Making sketches and plans for a gameboard and a rulebook, Lizzie called her invention The Landlord's Game.

The Landlord's Game

While living in Maryland in 1902, Lizzie finished up her board game and shared it with friends. The game focused on the buying up of land and being charged a single tax, or land value tax. Using a board and dice, players traveled a path made of squares that featured land, railroads, or utility companies up for sale. There were taxes to pay, a Poor House, a park, and a large private estate owned by Lord Blueblood, who would send a player to jail for trespassing. Lizzie's message was clear. The players began the game on a

---

28. Ibid

picture of a world map that featured the reminder: "Labor Upon Mother Earth Produces Wages."

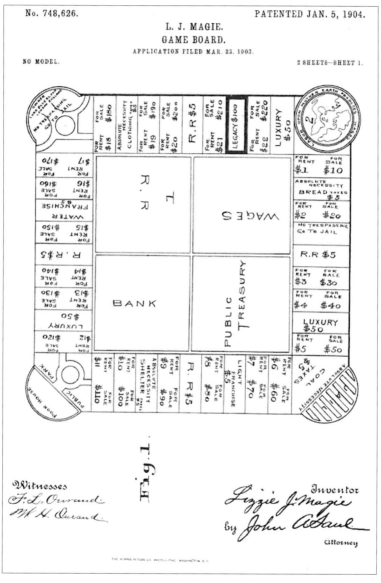

The 1904 patent for Lizzie Magie's game board that was later known as The Landlord's Game. Image courtesy of the Public Domain.

The game became wildly popular before Lizzie could apply for a patent. She was featured in a 1902 article in The Single Tax Review journal and quoted on her reasoning for the game:

> It is a practical demonstration of the present system of land-grabbing with all its usual outcomes and consequences... It might well have been called the 'Game of Life,' as it contains all the elements of success and failure in the real world...[29]

The review also included Lizzie's detailed explanation of some of the rules:

> Representative money, deeds, mortgages, notes and charters are used in the game; lots are bought and sold; rents are collected; money is borrowed (either from the bank or from individuals), and interest and taxes are paid. The railroad is also represented, and those who make use of it are obliged to pay their fare, unless they are fortunate enough to possess a pass, which, in the game, means throwing a double...

> Before the game begins, each player is provided with a certain amount of cash, sufficient to pay all necessary expenses until he is well enough along in life to earn his living. Should any one be so unlucky, or so reckless and extravagant, as to become 'broke,' there is a nice little poor house off in one corner where he may tarry until he makes a lucky throw or until some friend takes pity on him and lends him enough to set him on his feet again.

> The rallying and chaffing of the others when one player finds himself an inmate of the jail, and the expressions of mock sympathy

---

29. Miller, 1902

and condolence when one is obliged to betake himself to the poor house, make a large part of the fun and merriment of the game.[30]

The article and fascinating details of the game are irrefutable proof that the independent writer and reporter was the first to create the principles and rules of the Monopoly game that is still played today. Lizzie wanted people to understand the danger of land monopolies and the burden of multiple taxes on the middle class and poor. She felt the game was especially important for children:

> Children of nine or ten years and who possess average intelligence can easily understand the game and they get a good deal of hearty enjoyment out of it. They like to handle the make-believe money, deeds, etc., and the little landlords take a general delight in demanding the payment of their rent. They learn that the quickest way to accumulate wealth and gain power is to get all the land they can in the best localities and hold on to it. There are those who argue that it may be a dangerous thing to teach children how they may thus get the advantage of their fellows, but let me tell you there are no fairer-minded beings in the world than our own little American children. Watch them in their play and see how quick they are, should any one of their number attempt to cheat or take undue advantage of another, to cry, 'No fair!' And who has not heard almost every little girl say, 'I won't play if you don't play fair.' Let the children once see clearly the gross injustice of our present land system and when they grow up, if they are allowed to develop naturally, the evil will soon be remedied.[31]

---

30. Ibid
31. Miller, 1902

The patent for The Landlord's Game was applied for in 1903. Lizzie wrote that the game demonstrated "the present system of land-grabbing with all its usual outcomes and consequences."[32] She received a patent on January 5, 1904. It was tagged U.S. Patent 748,626, and three years later after moving to Chicago, Lizzie formed her own company, the **Economic Game Company**, to sell her board games.

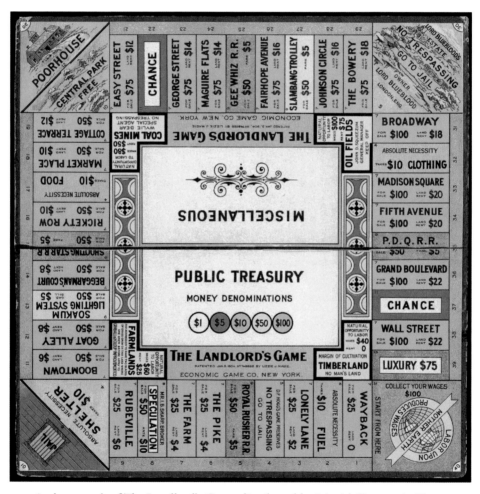

A photograph of The Landlord's Game distributed by Magie's Economic Game Company, New York. Courtesy of the Public Domain.

---

32. The Single Tax Review, 1902

Her game company was not the only game and toy business out there. Parker Brothers was a game company formed in 1883 by George Swinnerton Parker of Massachusetts. In 1910, Lizzie not only married Albert Phillips, she sold a card game to the Parker Brothers company called Mock Trial. Meanwhile, her Landlord Game idea was "borrowed" by a Scottish company called the Newbie Game Company and renamed the Bre'r Fox and Bre'r Rabbit game.

 Bre'r Fox and Bre'r Rabbit is an American folktale with roots mired in African slavery and emancipation that tells the story of a fox outwitted by a clever rabbit. It was made popular by the storyteller Joel Chandler Harris in a series of stories told by the imaginary Uncle Remus.

The main rules of The Landlord' Game continued to spread and become popular. Students played it at college with homemade boards and shared the game at home with the rest of the neighborhood. Frustrated at her lack of control over her own invention, Lizzie patented a new version of her game in 1924 under her married name, Elizabeth Magie Phillips. In 1932, she released it again in hopes of protecting her patent. The updated boardgame was now called Prosperity, and it featured street names on each square along the path to wealth. Prosperity was awarded patent number 1,509,312.

Even though she had patents to protect her creation, everyone played different versions of it and usually called it Monopoly. A college student in Reading, Pennsylvania copied it and renamed it Finance. A woman from New Jersey published a version of it with streets named from Atlantic City.

Then came the biggest insult of all: a man named Charles Darrow received a patent for an almost exact copy of Lizzie's game and sold it to Parker Brothers, the big game and toy company.

Playing Parker Brothers

At the beginning of the 20th Century — the early 1900s — the Industrial Revolution had changed family life for good. The working middle class, after fighting for fair treatment in the factories, had more time to relax and play games. Candles and gas-powered lights were being replaced by electricity. The radio spread news, a strange machine called the vacuum cleaner could replace brooms, and man had conquered the puzzle of flight at Kitty Hawk, North Carolina. Playing a boardgame that took luck, skill, and a little greed was a fun pastime.

In the early years of The Landlord's Game, a teacher at the University of Pennsylvania used the game in his economics class. Students took the ideas home. Teachers passed it on to friends and neighbors. Soon, the board design and the rules changed, as groups of players decided to allow properties not only to be rented, but auctioned out among the players. Buildings were added, and rent could be increased depending on how many there were on the property. The name changed, too. Players began to call the old Landlord boardgame Auction Monopoly. Soon, it was referred to just as Monopoly. The personal styles of homemade boards ranged from boards like the original Landlord Game to designs on fabric with properties drawn by hand — in crayon!

It became a source of pride and economics to keep the game simple and out of the hand of manufacturers. An editor of The Humanist wrote: "It was considered a point of honor not to sell it to a commercial manufacturer, since it had been worked out by a group of single taxers who were anxious to defeat the capitalist system."[33]

---

33. Dodson, 2011

In 1933, a man named Charles Darrow decided the game was worth too much to not sell, so he designed his own version. He offered it to game players in Philadelphia and then approached Parker Brothers. Within three years, the game Monopoly was the country's favorite pastime.

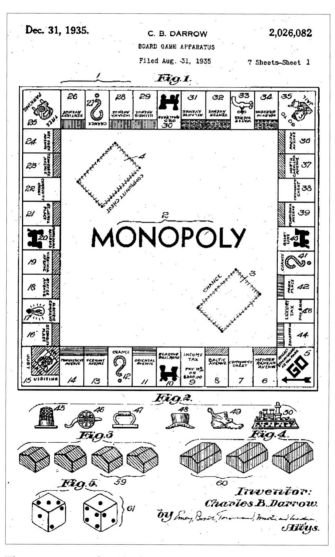

The 1935 patent for Charles Darrow's Monopoly board game.
Image courtesy of the Public Domain.

Lizzie was furious. Gathering her savings to pay for lawyers, she met with executives at the Parker Brothers company. They offered her $500 for her patent, but they wanted to keep the changes. Lizzie refused.

In court, a witness testified that she declared, "No. This is to teach the Henry George theory of single taxation, and I will not have my game changed in any way whatsoever."[34] Critics insisted she was too passionate about the Single Tax Law and the economic principles of Henry George.

The Parker Brothers company, which had published some of her earlier games, turned its back on her. The president of the company, Robert Barton, testified that they had only bought her earlier inventions to make her happy. He insisted that her version of The Landlord's Game was worthless to the company.

Lizzie went to the Washington Evening Star newspaper. Rather than back her cause, the newspaper revealed she had accepted $500, but it admitted the award did not come close to the money she had spent making the game, as well as buying the patent and the lawyers she hired to protect her copyright.

FAST FACT It was discovered that Elizabeth "Lizzie" Magie was the original inventor of Monopoly in 1973 when Professor Ralph Anspach of San Francisco University discovered her patents for The Landlord's Game. Professor Anspach had been sued by General Mills, who had bought Parker Brothers, for copying Monopoly when he applied for a patent for his own game, Anti-Monopoly. The professor of economics lost. After fighting Parker Brothers for 10 years, he was ordered to destroy thousands of his own boardgames. Professor Anspach published the truth about Lizzie and her boardgame and called the Charles Darrow story, "the Monopoly lie".

---

34. Ibid

Meanwhile, Charles Darrow became rich. He was given the official credit for creating Monopoly in his basement, but many of his friends and family knew the truth. He had first heard about the game from friends in Germantown, Pennsylvania.

Darrow's group of friends had been fellow students at the **Quaker Westtown School** in the early 1900s. One of his pals, a man named Charles Todd, reportedly shared the game with Charles Darrow and his wife. Charles Todd admitted later that when he shared the game with the Darrows, Charles asked him to write a copy of the rules, but these facts were buried in history, and the name Elizabeth Magie was forgotten for almost 100 years.

Lizzie died a childless widow in Arlington, Virginia in 1948. She never gave up on her belief that over-taxation held the poor and middle classes back. She published an essay in the Land and Freedom magazine eight years before her death. In the article, she warned her fellow Single Tax supporters,

> To simply know a thing is not enough. To merely speak or write of it occasionally among ourselves is not enough. We must do something about it on a large scale if we are to make headway. These are critical times, and drastic action is needed. To make any worthwhile impression on the multitude, we must go in droves into the sacred precincts of the men we are after. We must not only tell them, but show them just how and why.

Today, Elizabeth Magie is unofficially recognized as being the original creator of Monopoly. Although it had a different name and board design, her firm belief in herself as a woman of intelligence, business, and invention gave her the courage and means to seek out patents and produce educational entertainment for the masses at a time when very few women applied for patents.

Lizzie's large, sturdy tombstone sits under a tree in Columbia Gardens Cemetery in Arlington, Virginia. The engraved marker lists only her husband, her parents, and a grandmother. There is no mention of her successes or the game of Monopoly.

Chapter Six

More Ingenious Women

M any other inventive women created useful tools and machines in the earliest years of the Industrial Revolution. Some of them received patents, but some of the them did not seek them. They are still remembered today as pioneering women in American history.

Tabitha Babbitt And The Circular Saw

If you have ever cut wood, a shelf, or blocks to paint for crafting, you have probably used a power saw. A power saw is an electric, flat, circular blade with teeth around the edges. It's used by handy men and women, carpenters, cabinetmakers, and even hobbyists and do-it-yourselfers. Circular power saws are used to cut lumber or sheets of wood into smaller pieces, and they were invented by a woman in Massachusetts.

As early as the ancient Egyptians, wood was cut using axes and pull saws. The idea of using a thin blade to cut lumber dates back to at least the Medieval period, but it's believed that an invention was not officially recognized until 1777 when a British patent was issued to one Samuel Miller for a sawing machine. In America, the credit for the circular-shaped power saw first used in saw mills is given to a woman of the early Industrial Age known as Tabitha Babbitt.

Sometimes good ideas happen around the same time in different parts of the world. There is evidence that the Dutch invented a similar saw 100 years before Tabitha Babbitt. Another inventor built a circular saw in Germany in 1780.

Sister Tabitha Babbett was a Shaker. She was a devout, religious spinster who belonged to the Shakers of Harvard, Massachusetts. Her church members were known as The Lovely Vineyard. These industrious believers worked together to make and sell brooms and other household goods, and sold seeds and herbs, too.

 The Shakers were a religious group that broke off from the Quakers. They came to colonial America led by a sister named Ann Lee. The Shakers believed that men and women were completely equal, but that they should live separate lives without romance or marriage. They worshiped and worked together originally in industrious communities in New York, Massachusetts, Connecticut, and New Hampshire.

Tabitha was born in Massachusetts in 1784, less than 10 years after the Revolutionary War, to an unknown mother and a Thomas Babbitt. Tabitha was a spinner. Using a spinning wheel, she would have spun wool or cotton into thread. Old Shaker journals remember her as being inventive and clever.

Her first recorded idea for the Shaker community was the invention of cutting nails instead of making them by hand. The story goes that after watching a blacksmith make **wrought nails**, or handmade nails formed by hammering, she suggested using a sheet of iron. She believed that rolling an entire sheet of the metal into the thickness needed for the nails would be easier to work with because a blacksmith would only need to cut them off one by one. The idea worked.

Eli Whitney is also credited with inventing a nail-making machine.

In 1813, it is believed that Tabitha had her most successful idea of all after watching two men struggle to saw lumber with a **pit saw.** This type of saw only worked when it was pulled back and forth between two people. The labor was exhausting. The saw ripped up the lumber and only made cuts when it was pulled in a forward motion.

Tabitha went home to her spinning wheel and thought about it. She then explained that she made a tiny disc shape and notched it with sharp teeth around the edges. She attached it to her spinning wheel and tried to cut a piece of shingle. The invention worked, and Tabitha took it to the men cutting lumber in her community. She wouldn't apply for a patent; Shakers believed in humility and did not legally claim their inventions. Instead, they shared them with everyone.

A sketch of an early 20th century circular saw cutting wood.
Courtesy of Wikipedia Commons.

As good ideas do, the circle-saw principle spread fast through lumbering communities. The northeastern states of America thrived under lumber and textile production, and Tabitha's circular power saw, when attached to water wheels or steam engines, made cutting lumber easier and faster. Factories were built, ships were produced, and homes were crafted, all using lumber cut by Tabitha's forward-thinking machine.

"If the shakers were not the very first to use the circular saw, they were certainly early proponents."[35]

Tabitha died on December 10, 1858. She was buried at a Shaker community burial ground with only a simple marker. Despite the fact that she was a woman and would receive no money for her inventions, she continued to come up with creative solutions for the problems she saw around herself every day. At the time of her death, she was working on a set of false teeth. She left her project behind in a wax mold.

Martha Coston Lights Up The Navy

Not all fireworks are used for celebrations. In fact, one of the greatest advances in maritime safety and communication was the invention of signal flares at sea. They were first used during the Civil War and saved the lives of ship crews in stormy weather and in battle. The chemically-colored flares were a great advancement for the U.S. Navy.

The signal flares were the idea of an ingenious inventor named Benjamin Coston, but he died before he could figure out a way to make them work. The sketches were put away in a box until the love of his life, Martha, went searching for them.

---

35. Miller, 2010

Martha James Hunt was born in December of 1826. She was close to her large family of brothers and sisters, but more so, to her dear mother, who called her "Sunshine" for most of her life. Knowing the importance of education, Martha's widowed mother moved the family to Philadelphia, where Martha and her siblings studied and made friends.

While attending a social at 14 years old, she met her future husband, Benjamin Costin, at a pond, but since he was five years older, they could be nothing more than friends. Benjamin was already a well-known inventor devoted to science at 19 years old, and Martha wrote that she was awed "by his genius."[36]

Despite the age difference, Martha's mother allowed Benjamin to visit Martha on a regular basis. He inspired her to study harder, and she became head of her class even as she fell head-over-heels in love with him.

About this time, the famous admiral, "Old Ironsides," or **Admiral Charles Stewart**, encouraged Benjamin to go to Washington and present himself to the Secretary of the Navy. With the right introductions, he was quickly offered a job as head of the Navy laboratory in the Washington Navy Yard. There, Benjamin's inventions and solutions impressed the government so much he was ordered to accompany a two-year research expedition, but he did not want to leave Martha behind.

In 1842, Benjamin and Martha secretly eloped before he was to leave. Although they tried to keep it secret, word soon got out, and the young newlyweds had to confess to Martha's family. She was only 16 years old, but her mother already loved Benjamin so much that she forgave them both and gave her approval.

---

36. Coston, 1886

The Navy was not happy to learn that their scientist had decided to marry. Benjamin's expedition was cancelled, and he took Martha with him back to Washington. Martha's husband worked in a government **pyrotechnic** laboratory for several years before changing jobs and agreeing to experiment for the Boston Gas company.

The couple started a family in rapid succession, and by the time she was 21 years old, Martha found herself busy with four children. Benjamin was 26 years old, and the years of testing chemicals and gases may have taken a toll on his health. He became violently ill within a year of moving to Boston and died. No sooner had Martha moved in with her mother to mourn than one of her children became sick and passed away, leaving her futher heartbroken. A second child would die a few years later. She was a young widow and penniless, too.

> I knew not how to dig, I was ashamed to beg; and long and intently I pondered upon the course I should pursue, and earnestly I wished that nature had bestowed upon me a little of that brilliant genius so liberally given to my husband.[37]

As she struggled to find a solution to her poverty, Martha remembered a box of papers that her sick husband had told her were valuable and important. She searched until she found the small chest, and after reading through some of Benjamin's notes, decided his failed experiments with colorful firework flares might be valuable enough to sell to the Navy if she could improve them.

---

37. Ibid

"At last I came upon a large envelope containing papers and a skil[l]fully drawn plan of signals to be used at sea, at night, for the same purposes of communication that flags are used by day."[38]

The notes explained that the flares would explode in a certain order of colors, and that each flare would be assigned a number or letter in a signal book. One of the problems of Benjamin's tests was that the colors were not bright enough to see miles away and did not last long enough in the sky. Navy officials encouraged the idea, but after several failures, Benjamin had set the experiment aside.

Martha studied the papers and then wrote to a naval captain of her acquaintance to ask if he thought the nighttime signal flares would be something she could sell to the government. The officer did not reply, refused to meet with her, and avoided her letters demanding he return the notes and tests. Just as Martha was sure that her idea had been stolen, the captain was disgraced and forced to retire, and she wrote again, threatening to expose his theft if he did not give the experiments back. The man relented, and Martha snatched up her last hope to support her children and went to the Navy.

Officials approved of Martha's ideas and agreed to work with her to improve the technology. Another one of Benjamin's problems was that he had been working with the color blue, which did not work well with the other colors. After talking with chemists and conducting her own experiments, Martha realized that green worked best with red and white, and although they were not the colors of the American Flag, like Benjamin had wanted, the night signals worked and could be seen from four to 15 miles away.

---

38. Coston, 1886

After testing the flares shot with a pistol and having enormous success, several Navy officials wrote Martha letters of congratulations and gratitude. An order was made for $6,000. Martha quickly applied for a patent, #23,536, and in 1859, a year after her husband's death, the Pyrotechnic Night Signals were bought by the government for $20,000.

 Martha sold patents for her life-saving communication flares to England, France, Austria, Holland, Denmark, Italy, and Sweden.

Encouraged to take her patent to England and Europe, Martha became a very wealthy, single woman and traveled with her remaining two children all around the world. She sold her colorful night flares to shipyards, navies, sailing clubs, and governments. Kings and queens, and heads of state were anxious to meet and dine with her.

Martha even met Queen Victoria. She wrote about the first time she saw the short and plainly-dressed woman: "Who is that funny, fussy woman?" she asked her escort. The officer replied, "Good Heaven's Madame, that is our Gracious Sovereign!" Martha was impressed by Victoria's authority, especially after she loudly ordered all of the gentlemen to put on their hats when it began to rain.

Martha later created a twist-ignition device. Her thoughtful experiments and inventions aided the Navy during the Civil War in battle and blockades. They saved lives around the world at sea. The little schoolgirl from Philadelphia bravely turned her personal tragedies into triumphs that helped others and took her on expeditions of knowledge and adventures around the world.

When she died in Washington, D.C. at the age of 77, Martha Coston's remains were taken back to Philadelphia, where she was buried near the husband who had given her the courage to live.

An image of Martha Coston.
Courtesy of the Public Domain.

Mary And The Trains

New York City and other large cities are a little quieter and cleaner today thanks to Industrial-era daughter Mary Elizabeth. Born Mary Elizabeth Walton in 1827, Mary grew up with no brothers and a progressive father who must have believed in the education of young girls. The industrial era in New York had produced dirty factories and loud railroad tracks that polluted the air of the city, and the young girl knew nothing but noise and pollution. It must have affected her daily life.

As of January 2017, New York City has 665 miles of train tracks. If arranged in a single, straight line, these tracks would reach from New York City all the way to Chicago, Illinois.[39]

Like other heroines of the Industrial Revolution, Mary was a confident thinker who cared about finding solutions to help others. The problems of the Industrial Revolution became a main focus of her life, although we do not know why. Perhaps someone she loved struggled with breathing problems, or the sickness and diseases created by smokestacks and crowded streets caused deaths in her community that weighed heavily on her heart.

Regardless of the reason, Mary became an inventor and set her first sights on the noise caused by elevated railroad tracks that shook and rattled as the locomotives raced by. She lived by the Sixth Avenue railroad line, which must have been a loud, inconvenient location because she was inspired to do something about it.

Historical accounts tell stories of the young woman setting up a model train track in her basement to perform tests. Mary wanted to muffle the rattling noise made as locomotive wheels hit the sides of the tracks.

After trial and error, she created a system that used sand and cotton in wooden box-like trenches to quiet the ringing sounds. She applied for a patent on January 7, 1879. After receiving a patent for it in 1881, she sold it to the Metropolitan Railroad for a hefty $10,000.

The patent for the Elevated Railroad invention was classified as a, "Means for reducing the development or propagation of noise."[40]

---

39. Mta.info, n.d.
40. Walton, 1881

In the patent application, she confidently went on to explain how her invention would work:

> My invention has for its object the deadening or absorbing of the vibrations and noises made by the wheels of the cars as they roll over the tracks of elevated railways or railway-bridges; and, to this end my invention consists in certain combinations of the rails, the longitudinal guards, and the cross-ties with flooring and partitions, thus forming inclosures for bedding the rails in sand or such like materials, which smothers the noise, and when the sand is covered with asphalt the inclosed parts are protected from the weather. These combinations are specifically set forth at the end of this schedule.[41]

The rest of the patent application goes into specific detail for the construction of the noise reducing boxes so that city engineers would understand how to build them. After the Metropolitan Railroad picked up the design, other companies that built elevated railroads began to use the same invention.

Around the same time she was playing with trains, Mary worked on a way to cut down on the smoke puffing out of chimneys and factories. She created a way to pump smoke into water tanks to store the polluted air and its contents. The water in the tanks could then be emptied into city sewers instead of the air, cutting down on the greatest pollution problem America had ever known.

Mary applied for this patent in 1879, too. She was awarded the rights to her design in patent #221,880.

---

41. Ibid

The patent description describes her intentions and reasoning:

> ...preventing the escape of sparks, ashes, and impure or foul gases or vapors from the chimneys of locomotive-engines and from other chimneys into the atmosphere; and it consists in applying apparatus to or constructing chimneys substantially in the manner hereinafter.

> ...so as to cause the sparks, ashes, and impure gases or vapors which enter the chimney to be conducted into a tank containing water, or into the sewer, or to be otherwise disposed of, according to the description of furnace or the position of the chimney to which the invention is applied.[42]

Mary's inventions not only improved and probably saved lives in New York City, but they were also used in other cities, making her famous, appreciated, and wealthy. The amazing inventiveness and intelligence of her career was summed up in a women's magazine: "The most noted machinists and inventors of the century had given their attention to the subject without being able to provide a solution, when, lo, a woman's brain did the work..."[43]

During a time when very few women were given credit for their work, Mary was seen as a successful scientist and feminist. She became a national role model for other women of this period.

---

42. Ibid
43. Engineering.com, 2006

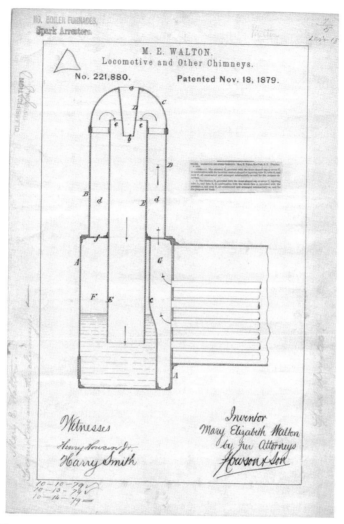

The 1879 patent for Mary Walton's invention to quiet the ringing of locomotive wheels. Courtesy of the Public Domain.

Josephine Cochrane's Dish Problem

Have you ever heard of the **Kitchen Aid** brand and all of its useful appliances? The roots of this company were formed in the 1880s when one woman grew tired of broken china.

The Industrial Age developed more than machines for factory work. In the middle of the late 19th century, a woman who took her social position in the community very seriously decided that something had to be done about her valuable china dishes. They were chipped every time a servant washed them. Her complaint and later determination to create an automatic dish washing machine made cleaning up after meals faster and easier for generations to come.

Josephine Cochrane was born in Ohio into a rather scientific family. Her father, John Garis, was a civil engineer. Her mother, Irene Fitch, was the granddaughter of **John Fitch**, the first inventor to be granted a patent for a prototype of a steamboat.

Not much of Josephine's education is known. She went to high school in Indiana and later moved to Shelbyville, Illinois to live with her married sister after their mother died. In Shelbyville, Josephine met a merchant named William Cochran. They married in October of 1858. According to history, Josephine added an "e" to the end of her married name to make it look more stylish.

The Cochran family of Shelbyville were successful and shared their good fortune with friends. They often threw parties and entertained visitors. They had enough money to hire servants, too, which meant Josephine did not have to spend any time in the kitchen, but that did not mean she did not treasure her china dishes. She claimed they were from the 17th century and that the servants were destroying them.

FAST FACT China dishes are made of porcelain, which is a type of clay heated at high temperatures to produce a delicate, bright white dish that can be decorated with painted designs. Marco Polo brought porcelain dishes from China after 1225 A.D. They became popular, especially for the wealthy, and were called china because of where they were made.

As her dishes came back to her chipped or broken following dinner parties, Josephine grew frustrated enough to wash them by hand herself. This kind of work was not something she was used to or enjoyed. She decided to create her own machine that would wash and dry them gently.

The idea had already been toyed with: in 1850, an inventor was granted the first patent for a dishwashing machine, but the slow, wooden, hand-cranked machine did not wash very well. Another patent was applied for in 1865, but this rack-style washer was still cranked by hand and did not become popular.

Josephine got to work in a backyard shed working on a model that would use water jets. It looked like a great idea, but her interesting hobby became serious business when Mr. Cochrane passed away unexpectedly, leaving her in debt. Josephine quickly went from the town socialite to the inventive widow determined to create and sell something useful.

Her design plans used racks with wired sections of specific sizes that fit cups, plates, or saucers. Everything would sit inside a copper boiler with a wheel that could eventually be powered by a motor. A local railroad mechanic named George Butters helped her build the first working machine, and they tested it in the Cochrane kitchen.

The first patent for the Cochrane Dishwasher was submitted at the end of December 1886, and Josephine organized her own company, calling it the Garis-Cochrane Dish-Washing Machine Company.

The Cochrane Dishwasher still used a hand crank, but the pressured pumps and jets along with the safety cage to hold dishes and utensils cleaned better than anything else that been invented before. After washing, hot, clean water could be poured over the dishes to rinse them, and they could sit and rest to dry. As the dishwasher model was improved, a self-rinse cycle was added and then a steam engine.

 The World's Fair is an event that showcases art and inventions from around the world. Different fairs, sometimes called expositions, can spotlight different scientific fields and cultures, and they usually welcome all people and cultures.

At first, Josephine's invention was only sold to restaurants and hotels. When the World's Fair was planned for Chicago in 1893, she took her dishwasher to the machine exhibition and won a prize for design and dependability. Nine different restaurants used the dishwasher at the fair, and its popularity spread. College campus kitchens and hospitals became interested, and Josephine's dishwasher began to be produced and sold from a company factory.

The Cochrane Dishwasher made life easier and cut down on chores for busy homemakers. In less than 100 years, women at home would prefer using machines instead of washing dishes by hand, and the dishwasher would be affordable and available to almost every family.

Josephine passed away in August of 1930. Her dishwashing company was bought by the Hobart Company, which eventually became the famous **Kitchen Aid** brand that you may know today. In 2006, she was welcomed as a member of the **National Inventors Hall of Fame,** more than 75 years after her death.

A poster for the 1893 World's Columbian Exposition (also known as the World's Fair) held in Chicago, IL. Image courtesy of the Public Domain.

Chapter Seven

The Glittering Girls of World War I

After the peak excitement of the Industrial Age, science, discovery, and the application of new ideas did not slow down. In the fields of chemistry and physics, new elements amazed even the scientists who discovered them. One leading woman in the field at the end of the 19th century was a French citizen known as **Marie Curie.** She would, quite literally, light up the world.

FAST FACT   A chemical element that gives off rays is radioactive.

Marie was a student at the University of Paris in 1897, and she decided to study **radiation**. Alongside her husband, Pierre Curie, she knew that atoms could be manipulated to give off invisible rays, like the X-rays discovered by **Wilhem Conrad Roentgen** in Germany. Elements were still being discovered, but now at a more rapid pace. In their 1898 laboratory, the Curies, along with another scientist, Gustave Bémont, discovered **polonium** and **radium**.

Two of us have shown that by purely chemical processes one can extract from pitchblende a strongly radioactive substance. This substance is closely related to bismuth in its analytical properties.

We have stated the opinion that pitchblende may possibly contain a new element for which we have proposed the name polonium.[44]

In her notes for radium, Marie added:

We believe nevertheless that this substance, although constituted for the greater part by barium, contains in addition a new element which gives it its radioactivity and which moreover is very close to barium in its chemical properties.[45]

Marie called her new element, "My beautiful radium." She was enchanted with it. Focusing her research on the amazing discovery, Marie was able to isolate radium within four years.

Radium Facts

Chemical element

Symbol: Ra

Atomic number: 88

Atomic mass: 226 u

Electron configuration: [Rn] $7s^2$

Radium appeared to have amazing potential because its rays could penetrate deep into matter before eventually breaking down. It would become infamous around the world, selling for what today would equal $2.2 million per gram. To understand the astounding price for such a small order, consider that a gram of sugar is less than one-fourth of a teaspoon!

---

44. Curie, 1898
45. Ibid

Radium Rocks the World

Before scientists and doctors really understood the power and consequences of using radium, the newspapers and science journals began to celebrate and encourage its use. Because its rays could enter the body and break down tissue, it was promised to cure cancer.

 Pierre and Marie Curie received the Nobel Prize in Physics in 1903, but they were both too ill to travel to the ceremony in Sweden. Pierre died in an accident in 1906, and Marie died in 1934, 23 years after winning a second Nobel Prize. Both recognized and recorded the dangers of exposure to radium, but their concerns were ignored by those who would profit from it.

By 1910, pharmacies and health-oriented companies created products with radium, believing it could help with mood, arthritis, aging, and overall health. The very wealthy bought expensive bottled radium waters. The new element was blended into chocolate bars and even put into bread. Toothpastes, makeup, and even spas offered radium in their natural products. Everyone was on board, even the toy companies.

Radium was special, not just because of the magical effects it was said to have on the body, but because when mixed with other materials it would glow. Toy manufacturers made night lights that lit up on their own, and the Radiumscope became a popular plaything for children to see how x-rays worked. It was given the nickname "liquid sunshine." Broadway wrote a song about it for the play, "Piff, Paff, Pouf", and called it "Radium Dance."

One of the most impressive uses for the glow-in-the-dark element was quickly applied to watches and clocks. Radium could be mixed into paint to make the painted numbers on clock faces glow at night so people could still tell time. With war on the horizon in 1916, it became obvious that paint and radium could entirely change battle strategies if applied to dials and timers on airplanes and tanks.

 World War I was an unprecedented bloody conflict between most of Europe. The Central Powers, composed of Germany, Austria-Hungary, and Turkey, fought France, Great Britain, Russia, Italy, and Japan. The United States joined in 1917. Over 116,000 Americans died, and twice as many were wounded for life.

America joined World War I in 1917. Radium now had an important and nation-saving purpose: it could save the lives of American soldiers, and it did. Radiation units were set up all over Europe where the wounded could have X-rays taken to see broken bones and bullets trapped in the body. Now someone was needed to paint the thousands and thousands of watches, clocks, and instrument dials that the soldiers would take into war. At the height of radium use during the years of 1917 to 1926, American women stepped up for the job.

Glittering Ghost Girls

Competition was tough for a job at the new watch-dial company in Orange, New Jersey. The factory, which the company called studios, was where women painted the numbers on watch faces by hand. The job paid well. The paint had radium in it, so the watches would glow in the dark.

The **Radium Luminous Material Corporation** opened in 1914 after creating the glow-in-the-dark paint called Undark. Owned by Dr. Sabin von Sochocky, who invented the paint using radium mixed with zinc sulfide, and Dr. George Willis, the company hired dozens of workers; by 1917, rocketing sales and the war kept the girls busy. So many girls loved the friends they made and the paychecks they earned that they got their sisters and other friends jobs at the factory, too.

The dial painters at the radium paint factories were in the top 5 percent of female wage earners in the country, taking home over $2,000 a year. Today that would equal around $43,000.

The painting process was tedious and required a steady hand. Bending their necks to see closely as they sat in single rows at long work tables, the workers each used a camel-hair brush with a tiny point. Upon training, they were taught to dip the brush into the powder, touch it to their lips to get a fine point, and paint over the numbers on the watch dials.

Originally, company records show that the brushes were dipped into water, but management felt it wasted too much of the expensive radium powder that collected in the bottom of the water dishes, so the dishes were removed.

Other factories opened in Illinois and Connecticut. Radium had been around for several years by now. The girls would have heard of it in their magazines or seen it advertised on beauty and toy flyers. Because it was celebrated as a wonder drug, most of the workers did not worry about being around it. In fact, they thought it was fun.

The fine, nearly invisible radium powder ended up everywhere. It drifted through the air and landed on hair, clothes, arms, legs, faces — even eyelashes. When the girls went into dark rooms, they glowed like fairies. Even after washing, their skin shimmered. One of the worker's husband later wrote that he could see his wife's apron where it hung on the wall at night and that it looked like a ghost!

This radioactive effect made the girls popular whenever they went out at night. Some of the workers would brush the powder over their makeup or add it to the expensive coats and shoes they were able to buy with their large paychecks. Under the city street lamps, they looked like fun-loving spirits and sprites. The appearance soon earned the girls nicknames like "the Ghost Girls" because they glittered and shined throughout every party.

A few of the girls did hesitate to put the radium-laced brushes into their mouths. One "radium girl" named Grace testified later in court that the Austrian company owner, Sabin von Sochocky, saw her touch the brush to her lips as he walked past her one day and commanded her to stop doing it.

Grace and the other early workers at the first factory in New Jersey did not know that creators of the paint knew it was probably dangerous. They did not know that one of the first scientists to work with radium, Marie Curie's husband, had said that he would not go near a room with pure radium because it would "burn all the skin off his body, destroy his eyesight, and probably kill him."[46]

After some of the girls began to feel achy and sick — and some even developed strange rashes and acne — they asked their bosses if the radium paint could be dangerous. The company said no. No one seemed to worry that many workers were getting the same kind of sores in their mouths.

There *was* someone who was concerned about the dangers of radium at the dial factories. The original inventor of the paint, von Sochocky, who had once warned a worker to keep a brush out of her mouth, had studied with the Curies. It is likely he had heard Thomas Edison's early warning that there may have not been enough time or study to know what the radium element would do as it broke down and aged.

The Austrian doctor had seen labs where the radium was manufactured and observed the workers wearing lead aprons for protection. He also would

---

46. Moore, 2017

have known that the rays given off did not just eat through tumors, but through any type of skin tissue. How could he not know? Sabin von Sochocky had his left fingertip amputated because radium had eaten through the flesh.

Eventually, von Sochocky left the company, and it became known as the **United States Radium Corporation**. Despite concerns from doctors treating company employees with the same or similar symptoms, and even an investigation by a government safety group, nothing was done to inform the glittering factory girls that the paint they used at work might harm them.

A photo of the Radium Dance Group. Courtesy of the Public Domain.

Sickness and death

The glittering ghost girls, some of whom started working as young as 14 years old, did not feel much like partying within a couple years of working with the radium paint. After the war ended, demand continued for a variety of glow-in-the-dark products people could use in the home. The girls continued to spend their days dipping brushes, touching them to their mouths, and painting. They spent the rest of their time feeling tired or sick. Some began to limp with leg or back pain, or develop lumps on their knees and legs.

One of the first shocking effects of working with the paint that raised alarms was that several of the girls began to experience tooth pain. Dentists and doctors began to see patients with loose or infected teeth. When a tooth was pulled, the hole left behind would not heal, but swell with gross infection and foul odors. Like a disease, another tooth would fall out, and so on. One dentist removed a tooth only to have a section of jawbone break into pieces.

Unknown to the workers and the medical community, the radium paint was eating through the teeth, jaws, mouths, and throats of the young women painting the radioactive dials — unless it decided to target other bones. Within four years of the first factory opening its doors, the first glittering ghost girl passed away.

Molly Maggia was the first to die. She endured losing her teeth, having her lower jaw removed, and then terrible throat pain. Molly passed away in 1922 at only 24 years old. The disease ate through the jugular vein in her throat, so she bled to death.

Young women who worked at the dial-paint factories began to die of mysterious bone-eating diseases. The company turned away investigators. No policy changes were made. The workers continued to dip and lick.

In the beginning, doctors believed it a was type of **phosphorous** poisoning; some even blamed the symptoms on **syphilis**. Regardless of the cause, the girls were enduring unbearable pain, but the company would not admit anything was wrong.

 In 1923, one year after the first victim, Molly Maggia, died of radium paint exposure from her workplace, the Radium Dial Company's top client controlled 60 percent of the alarm clock market.

Helen Quinlan died in 1923 at the age of 22. The disease that ate through her face and throat finally choked her to death. Then Irene Rudolph died of similar causes six weeks after her co-worker Helen. Irene was 21 years old.

The ghost girls knew it was not a coincidence they had all worked at the same place. After Irene Rudolph died, another young woman, Katherine Schaub, went to the Health Department in her New Jersey hometown. She reported the deaths in the early fall of 1923. Nothing was done. In that same year, one of the company founders, George Willis, had a thumb removed and discovered he had cancer. Although he no longer worked for Radium Dial, he knew there was a connection. Dr. Willis published a warning in a national medical journal. In his article, he said, "There is good reason to fear that neglect of precautions may result in serious injury to the radium workers themselves."[47]

More and more girls died. Catherine O'Donnell in December of 1923. Hazel Vincent Kuser died in agony on Christmas Eve in 1924. The radium

47. Moore, 2017

took its time eating through their bones, so they suffered unimaginable pain until their final moments.

The Big Fight

Grace Fryer was being eaten alive by radium from the inside out. She suffered in her foot, her spine, and eventually, like the others, in her jaw. In 1925, a New Jersey medical examiner ruled that the bodies of the radium factory girls he had examined had succumbed to anemia and disease by way of radiation exposure.

Grace had not worked with the radium-laced paint in two years, but she did not care what lawyers told her. A lawsuit had been filed in 1925 by a coworker, but the case had dragged out and the victim, Marguerite Carlough, had died.

Grace filed a lawsuit anyway, asking for $1.7 million. Four other workers joined the cause, including Katherine Schaub, who had tried to raise the alarm after the deaths of Helen Quinlan and Irene Rudolph.

The enormous lawsuit finally did something that the funerals did not do. The newspapers got ahold of the story, and suddenly, the fading ghost girls of World War I who had danced away the nights of their late teens and early 20s, had the power and the resources to share their stories of injustice and company greed — just in time before they died. Like zombies, they would become known as the Living Dead.

The trial and its shocking testimony of lies and coverups, along with its graphic witnesses and photographs of death, could have been the trial of the century. Scientists and health inspectors who had been ignored, threatened, or bribed, came forward to tell the truth. The defense was preparing a shattering bombshell.

Because the exposure and deaths had taken place in two different places and information had been hidden, it had taken time for the truth to be recognized and revealed. The grave of the first victim, Molly Maggia, was reopened. Her remains tested positive for radium exposure. In fact, they glowed. Around this time, another ghost girl passed away of a disease that turned her face black and infected her entire head.

The radium company, now the United States Radium Corporation, did everything in its power to delay the trial and avoid accepting any responsibility, possibly waiting for the victims to hurry up and die. Its factory in New Jersey closed in 1927. In 1928, the inventor of the glow paint, von Sochocky, died from his years of exposure to radium. Seventeen girls, as far as it was known, had already passed away from his invention.

Under public and government scrutiny, the United States Radium Corporation had no choice but to proceed after stalling the trial for five months. Hoping to avoid a media circus, they offered a little cash to the victims, but it was refused.

Experts came forward. More lawsuits were filed that proved radium exposure could be deadly. When there was irrefutable evidence presented that the company had known for certain of the dangers of radium at least as early as 1925, the lawyers surrendered and offered each victim a cash sum of $10,000. The New Jersey factory was destroyed and paved over.

Grace and the others accepted, but they did not really win. After paying for her medical bills, there was little left behind to leave for her family. She would die on October 27, 1933.

Katherine Schaub, who had courageously fought to expose the truth, died on February 18, 1933, after years of suffering from an infection in her leg. Her father died a week later.

The United States Radium Corporation had known of the dangers. They had done their own tests and hired their own investigators. Reports and knowledge were kept secret while more girls were hired to handle the radium paint and put out products. The money they paid out to the victims was a trivial amount to the millions they made in their studios. But if they thought the business was over and done, they were wrong.

A mystical image of a man holding a jar that supposedly contains radium.
Courtesy of the Public Domain.

One More Girl

Catherine Wolfe was born in 1903 in Ottawa, Illinois. She was thrilled to get a job as a young woman painting dials at the Illinois location that opened after the first studio in New Jersey. Catherine was working at the Ottawa studio during the publicized lawsuit between the first dial painters who joined forces and went to court. She was concerned.

In Ottawa, Illinois, Catherine and her workers were told there was no such thing as radium poisoning. When production slowed down because of fears and suspicion, the girls were tested. Catherine later testified that they were not allowed to see the results. They were jokingly told by their male superiors that radium would make them more attractive and give them "rosy cheeks."

Catherine became ill in 1929. She limped and sometimes fainted. Her co-worker, Peg Looney, had already died. Then another joined her, Mary Tonielli. Catherine married in 1932 and had a son. Around her, more women who had painted with her at the Ottawa studio became ill or died. No one seemed to want to admit what was wrong, but Catherine knew.

Catherine Wolfe was now Catherine Donohue. She grew sicker and sicker and watched her family finances collapse under the strain of so many medical bills. Angry at the denial of the company's responsibility, she filed a new lawsuit. The community did not believe her. The doctors claimed to be confused. At first, no lawyer would take her case. Another lawsuit in New Jersey was defeated.

By 1938, Catherine had an enormous tumor on her hip. Her lawyer, Leonard Grossman, took her case for free. He sat at her bedside and recorded her testimony for trial while she fought to hang on. She had endured years of doctor visits and six different operations. Her final pregnancy she had endured without taking any painkillers so she could save her child. Her jaw was infected and her teeth were falling out.

Incredibly, the United States Radium Corporation had won a few additional lawsuits where blame on the radium paint could not be proven. They claimed any type of radium poisoning was a phase. They insisted workers were not trained to put the paint brushes into their mouths.

Catherine gathered witnesses and gave explicit details of everything she could remember. During one moment in the trial, she broke down into tears when a doctor said she would not live. For her final act of courage, she took the stand and held up a piece of her diseased jaw that had been removed.

Finally, the trial ended with a guilty verdict. The United States Radium Corporation fought it, but they lost. They were ordered to award Catherine $12,000, but they appealed again. Her lawyer, Grossman, spoke out, declaring that he just couldn't imagine "a friend fresh from the profoundest depths of perdition committing such an unnatural crime as the Radium Dial Company did. My God!"[48]

Catherine died on July 27, 1938 at a weight of only 60 pounds. Her trial had made the news with pictures in the newspapers. The radium company lost its last appeal. The girls had finally won.

 A few of the ghost girls who worked for the dial painting company did live longer than most of the early victims. Merced Reed died of colon cancer in 1971. Charlotte Purcell lived to 82 after having her arm amputated. One lived to be 92, and miraculously, another died after turning 98.

---

48. Moore, 2017

Just as greed took the lives of factory workers at the dawn of the Industrial Revolution, the love of money and power superseded any compassion or concern the manufacturers of radium-painted products had for the workers, mostly women, who sat side by side as they worked long shifts for a salary they could not afford to turn down.

> "Now, even our crumbling bones
> will glow forever in the black earth."[49]

Today, the resting places of the glittering ghost girls of World War I still give off radiation that can be identified using a **Geiger counter** at their gravesites.

---

49. Swanson, 2002

Chapter Eight

Fight Club

Unions

They were not actually boxing during the Industrial Revolution, but, like the first young women at Lowell Mill, women of the period had learned the hard way that they would have to fight for the individual and civil rights of their sex. Women learned how to organize and formed their own "fight clubs" to fight for what they felt was equal and fair treatment.

Society still functioned by assigning the idea of a **living wage** to men and expecting women to work exclusively in the home. This created a problem for young women who had grown up at the dawn of revolution for industry and labor that would hire and pay a female. They wanted to work, they knew they had to organize, and over the decades, they learned how to fight legislatures and public opinion for equality. The seeds of women's rights today were planted by some of these earliest organizations to protect women and worker rights.

In the month of June 1900, thousands of factory workers joined together and formed the International Ladies' Garment Workers' Union. They fought for fair hours and wages and joined other working men in strikes and other political acts of rebellion in the name of solidarity.

The International Ladies' Garment Workers' Union was shortened to the ILGWU. Most of the first members were Jewish workers from New York who suffered in factories operating under dangerous conditions.

Female shirtwaist factory workers on strike. Photo courtesy of the Public Domain.

The first delegates were representatives of 11 unions in New York, Pennsylvania, Maryland, and New Jersey. They represented about 2,000 workers, mostly comprised of Eastern European immigrants.

Ironically, the first president of the ILGWU was a man by the name of Herman Grossman. They chartered four of the first seven unions to attend the meetings and later added groups from Illinois, Ohio, Michigan, and even California.

In the early years of the organization, membership repeatedly participated in meetings, lawsuits, strikes and bargaining. In 1907, 1,200 reefer-makers walked out until agreements were made for lower the required hours for the work week and to allow help for workers who had complaints or issues. A group of members, called an arbitration board, was formed to work out labor disputes between workers and management. That same year, 2,000 workers in the Boston garment industry went on strike demanding similar rights.

> **FAST FACT** On March 25, 1911, a fire caused the deaths of 146 men and women at the Triangle Shirtwaist Factory in New York City. Because doors were locked and the fire escapes were broken, not everyone could evacuate the building. It was the deadliest industrial factory tragedy in New York and was answered with new and powerful regulations and inspections for the workplace.

Not long after, the ILGWU organized two more successful strikes in 1909 and 1910 that won higher pay and shorter hours. The "Uprising of the 20,000" included women shirt makers in New York City, and the strike made progressive leaps in reassuring workers' rights for women. It resulted in an agreement called the **Protocol of Peace**. This agreement set up committees for sanitation, complaints, and arbitration.

The ILGWU found and promoted the Liberal political party in the state of New York. It later would spread its mission to the unification of art, education, health care, and equal housing. As clothing factories eventually shifted overseas over 50 years later, the ILGWU merged with the Union of Needletrades, Industrial and Textile Employees in 1995.

Today, more women belong to unions than ever before. In the past 30 years, female membership in unions has risen from 34 to 46 percent.[50] Thanks to their sisters who organized and fought for fair treatment during the Industrial Revolution, they earn more than non-union female employees in every state and enjoy job safety and arbitration protection.

---

50. Iwpr.org, 2018

Suffrage

The right to vote in an election is called suffrage. Originally, only white males were allowed vote for government leaders or decisions in American elections. Other men, including men of color, were given the right to vote in 1870. Although women were already campaigning for voting rights decades before the Civil War, they were denied that opportunity until 1920.

During the early 1800s, as women entered the industrial workforce, unions were not the only place they could organize. Many championed or joined groups to support religious and moral clubs, temperance — or avoiding alcohol — movements, and anti-slavery organizations.

Before the suffrage movement was fully organized, several Western states pioneered the idea that American women were equal to men and passed early legislation that allowed their female citizens voting rights. The first was Wyoming in 1890; Colorado followed in 1893, then Utah and Idaho in 1896.

Susan B. Anthony is one of the most famous women of the age who helped women organize to win the right to vote. She was born in 1820 in Massachusetts and raised as a Quaker. After becoming a teacher, she joined temperance groups and anti-slavery efforts. She realized that women could not really have a political voice unless they could vote. In 1866, she co-founded the American Equal Rights Association and published The Revolution newspaper out of New York.

Many suffrage organizations differed on how to organize and campaign. While Susan's movement focused on changing the constitution, others, like the American Woman Suffrage Association, focused on winning voting rights state by state.

An old postage stamp promoting women's suffrage.
Image courtesy of Shutterstock.com.

Suffragettes endured criticism and were called radical. Some endured abuse and arrest. After a period of almost 70 years, the 19th Amendment was ratified and added to the Constitution on August 26, 1920, allowing all American women the right to vote.

Although the 19th amendment gave American women the right to vote, black and other minority women still struggled to be heard. The first national organization for women of color was formed in 1896. Known as the National Association of Colored Women, it focused on its motto, "Lifting as we climb" and worked to show the rest of the world that African-American women had the same goals and interests as others leading women's and equal rights.

Guides and Scouts

Women in the latter-half of the Industrial Revolution encouraged their daughters to step up and take advantage of new opportunities. During World War I, with so many men overseas, sisters, mothers, and wives took on more responsibilities. Children needed a way to be supportive and productive, too. Clubs like the **Campfire Girls**, **Girl Scouts**, and **4-H** were organized.

 The Campfire Girls were formed in 1910 in Maine. The goal of the organization was to be a sister group to the Boy Scouts of America, teaching mostly domestic life skills and patriotic duty to young American women.

Girl Scouts of America was formed in 1912 in Savannah, Georgoa. Its founder, Juliet Gordon Low, had met the founder of the Boy Scouts, Robert Baden-Powell, in London and wanted something similar for American girls. It was first called the Girl Guides of America. The group provided a way for girls to practice domestic and outdoor skills and to learn to become independent and self-reliant. In 1913, the name was changed to Girl Scouts. Girl Scouts helped sell war bonds and participated in other patriotic duties during World War I, including raising funds or contributing supplies to the Red Cross.

 Clara Barton founded the American Red Cross branch from the International Red Cross in 1881 after her years of serving as a nurse in the Civil War. In Virginia, she was knowns as the "angel of the battlefield."

Women in the Military

More than a century later, historians debate the impact the Industrial Revolution had on women. Some believe the loud, steaming factories provided work and higher wages than the cottage industry. Others believe that females, especially in the countryside, suffered as skilled jobs and the ability to sell goods moved to the cities.

American women enjoy more opportunities and have more rights today than any of their early colonial sisters. However, those early years of American history during the Industrial Revolution cracked open doors into the heart and mind of society and offered a way and an opportunity for change. It was a slow but steady march that began with inventive women, hard-working and ambitious women, and female warriors brave enough to defend these ideas — and their country.

The War of Independence

Traditionally, women have stood in the background of military affairs. During the American Revolutionary War (1775-1783), when the colonies fought for independence from the British Crown, women served in the camps with special permission. Many wives followed their husbands because they had no choice, others served out of a sense of duty, determination, and courage. In the tented villages that housed the rebel soldiers, women washed and mended laundry or cooked. Others who were qualified were allowed to serve beside doctors as nurses. Those who wanted to fight, however, had to dress in disguise. Believe it or not, this happened more than many believed.

Deborah Sampson was one of those industrious colonial women. Born in 1760 in Massachusetts, she was sent from her widowed mother to work as an indentured servant. Deborah worked hard, educated herself, and then went to work.

Whatever Deborah saw during the early years of the American Revolution must have awakened some sense of duty in the young woman. She was tall, broad, and strong, known for being mechanically creative. It was the perfect formula for disguising herself and entering the war.

Deborah enlisted, or signed on, as a male soldier to fight in the war in 1782. She was caught the first time before she was sent to battle but signed up again under the name Robert Shurtleff and was assigned to the Fourth Massachusetts' Company of Light Infantry. Her job was to scout for enemies. On one mission, she was forced to fight "man" to man in a skirmish with enemy soldiers. For the last two years of the war, she led raids and fought under cannon fire.

 Two women, Mary Marshall and Mary Allen, were invited to serve as nurses about the *USS United States* during the War of 1812 between the United States and Great Britain.

The Revolutionary warrior hid her true gender for almost two years. Her secret was discovered when she became so sick she had to be taken to a hospital. Although her husband later had to pay for her pension, the military did not punish her, but instead gave her an honorable discharge. Deborah became one of the most infamous women to fight for American independence and the first to tour the country as a public speaker. At some events, according to history, she wore her military uniform.

The Civil War

At the height of the Industrial Revolution, the war between the American northern and southern states began. The Civil War began in 1861 and would last four more years. The idea of women in battle was still unthinkable, but society recognized that with so many men sacrificed on the battlefields, women could fill roles alongside doctors and cooks. Some women were permitted to serve in hospital administration. Others pursued ways to serve more inconspicuously as spies.

Hundreds of women risked their lives and families to become spies during the Civil War. One of them, Harriet Tubman, became the first American woman to lead a military mission.

A portrait of Harriet Tubman.
Courtesy of the Library of Congress.

Born a slave in Maryland, Tubman is famous for her service to the **Underground Railroad**. After running away to freedom in 1849, she made a recorded 19 trips over a period of 10 years to free slaves, including some of her own family. They traveled at night by following the North Star. The fearless and courageous woman carried a gun that she was not afraid to use. She did not allow deserters.

At the start of the Civil War, Harriet volunteered as a cook and nurse. The military, aware of her history, courage, and intelligence, asked her to serve as a spy. Harriet organized a spy ring of former slaves in South Carolina. She led a raid with Colonel James Montgomery to free slaves who worked along the Combahee River, a small waterway in the lowlands of South Carolina. During the mission, she helped soldiers plant mines and destroy a supply depot. Her efforts freed over 700 in slavery.

Harriet received a monthly pension after her husband passed away, but she was never awarded financially for her service, although the military granted her honors at her burial. In 2003, Congress finally awarded $11,750 to the Harriet Tubman Home in Auburn, New York for her selfless and revolutionary service.

 Elizabeth Newcom joined a Missouri infantry unit disguised as a man during the Mexican-American War (1846-1848). She marched about 600 miles until she was discovered in Colorado and dismissed.

The World Wars

The continued industrialization of America led to revolutionary roles and more opportunities for women. When World War I was declared in 1917, women found that once-closed doors were finally open wide enough for a female to march through if she chose. Although they were not allowed to have military title or rank, they served overseas for the first time. Women served in transportation and nursing. During the war, over 33,000 women volunteered. More than 400 would sacrifice their lives beside their male counterparts.

The Donut Girls of World War I

Sometimes they baked within just a few miles of the front lines, but a special group of volunteer women during the First World War learned how stay safe while comforting others with just basic supplies they scrounged up around the camps. The Donut Girls initially served soldiers with music and religious services, but that changed in the fall of 1917 when two women, Margaret Sheldon and Helen Purviance, discovered that they could make donut dough with leftover rations of flour, sugar, and lard. Wine bottles and even shell casings became rolling pins, and empty helmets were used as pots to fry the donut dough. Some days, they cooked over 2,000 of these treats to serve with hot chocolate. Sometimes they had enough ingredients to make cakes and pies, too. The service not only made sponsoring the Salvation Army look good, the sweet treats comforted and encouraged the troops who often wrote home about the one luxury in the middle of battle that gave them moments of happiness.

World War I Donuts

Ingredients:

5 cups of flour
2 cups of sugar
5 teaspoons of baking powder
1/4 teaspoon of salt
2 eggs
1 3/4 cups of milk
Grease to fry donuts

Directions:

Combine all ingredients to make the dough. Knead dough, roll it smooth, and then cut it into circles. Fry donuts in oil until brown. Dust with sugar or cinnamon.

Yield: 4 dozen

The service of women after World War II solidified their presence in the United States military. Congress passed the Women's Armed Services Integration Act in 1948, allowing all women service opportunity in the military. It included benefits.

Later, over 50,000 women would serve in Korea aboard ships or in combat hospitals between 1950-1953. During the Vietnam War (1954-1975), women volunteered to serve in all branches of the military. By 2015, 15 percent of the United States military was made up of women.[51] They served everywhere, from the infantries to the officers' quarters.

 More than 400,000 women served their country during World War II. They drove ambulances, worked as mechanics, and even flew planes. Over 80 female military personnel were captured as prisoners of war.

Skirts and Politics

Organizing unions and the fight for civil rights naturally led some women into politics. Although it would be near the close of the Industrial Revolution before the first woman would achieve winning a mayoral election in 1862, many notable women entered the political arena in their petticoats and long skirts.

 Mary Wollstonecraft is one of Great Britain's first women's rights activists. She wrote and campaigned in England during her life between 1759 and 1797. She wrote "A Vindication of the Rights of Woman," which argued that women were born equal to men. The book was used by many American women who fought for civil and political equality. A woman of her word, Mary infamously kidnapped her own sister and niece to rescue them from a poor home and family situation.

---

51. History.org, 2008

Lucretia Mott

Lucretia Mott loudly rallied women to fight against slavery and pursue the right to vote. She was raised in a Quaker family in Massachusetts, believing that men and women of all color were born equal and entitled to freedom.

Although she was the mother of a large family, Lucretia joined her husband in supporting the American Anti-Slavery Society. She wrote and spoke publicly about her beliefs, branding herself as an unacceptable advocate of her sex.

In 1840, she met Elizabeth Cady Stanton, another activist, and together they organized the **Seneca Falls Convention** to promote women's rights. The convention demanded the right to vote and the right of women to divorce, retain custody of their children, and own property.

 Elizabeth Cady Stanton (1815-1902) helped organize the women's suffrage movement with Susan B. Anthony. She is remembered for her battle to alter the 14th and 15th Amendments to guarentee both men and women, regardless of color, the right to vote.

The Motts continued to fight to end slavery, lecturing against the **Fugitive Slave Act** passed in 1850. Lucretia became the first president the **American Equal Rights Association** (**AERA**) and fought for equal rights of all women and men, regardless of color. She died in 1880, a leader of the women's suffrage movement.

Harriet Beecher Stowe

Harriet Beecher Stowe lived between 1811 and 1896. Raised by for-ward-thinking parents, she was encouraged to read, write, and pursue higher education. Sympathetic to the anti-slavery movement, she was devastated after her toddler son died and was inspired to explore the cruelty and grief experienced by enslaved parents separated from their children. Rather than march or lecture, Harriet turned to the power of the pen.

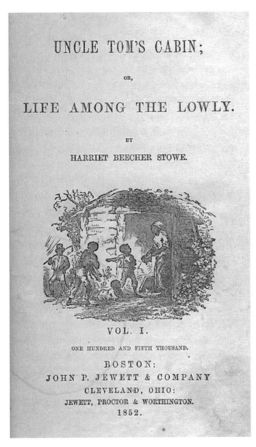

The title page of an 1852 edition of Harriet Beecher Stowe's "Uncle Tom's Cabin." Image courtesy of the Public Domain.

1n 1851, Harriet published "Uncle Tom's Cabin" to denounce the evils of slavery and its contradiction to Christian principles. The book told the story of a slave named Tom who is separated from his family and becomes friends with Eva, a white plantation owner's daughter. Before he can be freed from slavery through Eva's wishes on her deathbed, he is beaten to death for helping slaves escape. The book sold over 10,000 copies in its first week.[52]

Harriet's beliefs and literary activism helped change the way many Americans felt about slavery and opened their minds to the idea that all men were equal, regardless of color or background.

Dorothea Dix

Dorothea Dix became a political advocate for women, the mentally ill, and prisoners while working as a teacher and author. She was born in Hampden, Maine in 1802 to strict parents who struggled with depression and alcohol. Because of this, Dorothea became the mother of the family, taking care of everyone else while reading voraciously to educate and prepare herself for the future.

When she was 12 years old, Dorothea moved to Boston to live with her grandmother. She received the education she must have hoped for during the lonely, demanding years of her childhood and went on to become a teacher and open six different schools.

After a bout of illnesses, Dorothea went to England and returned with an awareness and desire to work for better care in insane asylums and educational opportunities in prisons. She taught in the East Cambridge jail in Massachusetts and began to speak out about the abuse of prisoners and the problem of mixing the criminals with the mentally insane. She visited several more prisons and took her reports of abuse and neglect to the Massachusetts State Legislature.

---

52. History.com, 2009

Because of Dorothea's work, courage, and brutal honesty, money was earmarked for a state hospital for the mentally ill, and the public was better educated on what needed to be done for the imprisoned to be treated with humanity. The movement spread to surrounding states.

"You never saw a very busy person who was unhappy."[53]

—Dorothea Dix

At the beginning of the Civil War, hospitals suffered under much of the same conditions Dorothea had seen in prisons and asylums. In 1861, she was asked to organize Union hospitals for wounded soldiers and was appointed as the superintendent of female nurses. Her blunt way of dealing with inefficiency influenced her administration by turning other women against her while insulting and irritating Union officials. In the fall of 1863, two years before the war's end, Dorothea was asked to leave, and she returned home. She continued to speak, write, and teach how to organize and treat patients in different institutions.

The little girl with the soft heart for the troubled or confused left behind a legacy of a redesigned hospital system that redefined health care during the Industrial Revolution. She lived to be 85 years old, passing away in 1887 in a New Jersey hospital.

Local and Federal Office Firsts

If you have ever wondered when women were first elected to political positions, it is interesting to know that the first female representative in the U.S. House of Representatives was a Montana woman by the name of

---

53. Medina, 2018

Jeannette Pickering Rankin. She was elected before women won the right to vote in national elections.

FAST FACT The first woman to win a mayoral election in a United States town is believed to be Nancy Smith of Oskaloosa, Iowa. It was 1882, and she declined the position. The first woman to become a mayor in the United States is recorded as Susanna Madora Salter of Argonia, Kansas in 1887.

Jeannette was born in Montana in 1880 and was educated at the University of Montana in 1902. She fought for women and the right to vote by serving in the National American Woman Suffrage Association (NAWSA). Her determination and political skills helped Montana women win the right to vote early in 1914.

She ran for a house seat to represent Montana in 1916 and won. Afterward, she declared, "I may be the first woman member of Congress, but I won't be the last."[54]

Jeannette went on to protest wars and promote peace, holding office again in 1942. She died in 1970 when she was 93 years old.

54. History.house.gov, 2018

Chapter Nine

Post-War Innovative Women

Diaper Duty

After World War II, an intelligent, successful woman named Marion O'Brien Donovan left an editing job at the popular magazine Vogue to become a full-time mother and homemaker. Ambitious and creative, she was born with entrepreneurial roots. Her father and uncle worked in manufacturing and were inventors. As a girl growing up in Fort Wayne, Indiana during the 1920s, she spent time around her family as they invented factory machines, like an industrial lathe, a machine for shaping metal or wood into parts.

Educated at Rosemont College in Pennsylvania, Marion settled down in Connecticut to raise her three children. Dealing with wet baby bottoms that caused rashes and soaked through furniture, Marion decided there was room for improvement in the homemaking industry and put her mind to work. One day, after noticing the waterproof qualities of her shower curtain, she realized there was a better way to diaper and protect a baby.

The Industrial Revolution had advanced improvements for business and manufacturing, but nothing had been invented to improve cloth diapers. At the time, babies and young children were swaddled in pieces of cotton that were pinned together and then covered with a pair of rubber pants.

The rubber covers did not allow absorption or air flow, so painful diaper rash was a common problem, not to mention leaks. Marion took her shower curtain inspiration and tried sewing a simpler solution with her sewing machine. Eventually, she created a plastic outer covering that mothers could slide cloth diapers into for moisture-proof protection.

A 1937 photo of women folding cloth diapers. Courtesy of the Library of Congress.

The boat-shaped diaper cover had snaps, which eliminated the need for sharp safety pins, and allowed more air circulation than rubber pants. It worked for her children, so Marion took the idea to manufacturing companies. The baby industry had no interest. Manufacturers told the inventor there was no need for such a thing. Of course, Marion disagreed. With her own knowledge and family experience in manufacturing, she decided to produce it herself. She took an order to Saks Fifth Avenue in 1949, and the company couldn't keep the Boaters on the shelves.

 One baby will use approximately 6,000 diapers within the first two years of life.[55]

In 1951, Marion wisely applied for a patent for her diaper covering. After receiving it, she sold it for $1 million. She took her money and ideas and started working on an even better idea: the disposable diaper.

The disposable diaper could be bought, used, and then thrown away. It eliminated laundry and protected the baby from pins and diaper rash. Marion took her improved diapering invention to the baby industry again and was surprised to be turned down for lack of interest. 10 years later, a chemical engineer by the name of Victor Mills, with the Procter & Gamble company, created his own version of the modern disposable diaper and called it Pampers. Successful in marketing and branding, it became a world-wide bestseller.

Marion continued to invent. She applied for patents for a soap dish insert, a closet hanger system, and dental floss. In all, she received over 20 patents in her lifetime and an architectural degree from Yale which she used to design her own house. Marion passed away in New York City in 1998. She was inducted into the National Inventors Hall of Fame in 2015.

Bulletproof

If you know someone who works as a first responder or is in the military, you can thank Stephanie Kwolek for the life-saving, bullet-proof vests, helmets, and other Kevlar equipment that they wear.

---

55. Realdiapers.org, n.d.

Kevlar helmets are 40 percent more resistant to impact than metal helmets.[56]

Stephanie Kwolek is the renowned DuPont chemist who invented the light but strong-as-steel polymer identified as I-4B, or **Kevlar**. One of the first women to work for DuPont following World War II, Stephanie was born in New Kensington, Pennsylvania. Her mother taught her how sew and design, and her father shared his knowledge of the outdoors with her. Stephanie grew up exploring these creative outlets by designing clothes, making field guides of the trees and plants around her home, and reading all kinds of scientific books.

A perfectionist, Stephanie excelled in school. She could remember almost everything she read and was better at math than most of the boys in her classes. Interested in a variety of sciences, she attended Carnegie Mellon University, where she studied chemistry under both male and female professors. She liked studying under intelligent, proactive women and was inspired to pursue medicine. After graduation, she applied for a job as a chemist with the DuPont Company and embraced the opportunity to research with **polymers.**

Polymers are large molecules that are made of up similar or repeating units that form microscopic chains. These molecules can form synthetic, or imitation, organic materials. For example, plastic is a synthetic material.

Working with polymers was so interesting that Stephanie decided to stay with DuPont and gave up her ambition of being a doctor. She liked being able to research and work alone. Experimenting with chemicals and searching for discoveries satisfied her thirst for knowledge and her desire to be creative.

---

56. Sciencehistory.org, 2017

In the lab, Stephanie worked on projects like developing new condensation processes that would work at lower temperatures. In the late 1960s and early 1970s, fuel crises crippled the country, and DuPont challenged its scientists to find a polymer lighter than steel that could be used to make tires.

Experimenting with synthetic polymers of high molecular weight, Stephanie made a discovery. Rod-like **polyamides**, made of polymers, lined up and formed liquid with crystals. She wondered what spinning the solution would do, but at first, the engineer in charge of spinning refused to test it. He told her the tiny crystal particles would jam up his machine. After a few days, the worker relented, and Stephanie spun the experiment, much like sugar is spun into cotton candy. It produced long, light fibers that were remarkably strong. The yellow super fiber was called Kevlar, and DuPont, along with Stephanie's research, discovered over 200 uses for it.

Kevlar is used in fiber optics. It is woven into fabric and lines equipment like helmets and the bulletproof vests that police officers wear. It can be added to clothing, household goods, and auto products.

 Kevlar is used in luggage, socks, shoes, gloves, tires, cables, truck bed liners, skis, boats, armored cars, and more. Because it stretches and distributes force on impact, rather than give way, it has saved countless lives.

In 1986, Stephanie retired as a DuPont researcher. She was inducted into the National Inventors Hall of Fame in 1994 and recieved, among other honors, the National Medal of Technology in 1996. In 2014, this post-Industrial Revolution thinker passed away in Delaware at the age of 90. She was a mentor to other female scientists during her lifetime and is a role model to other women in the field of chemistry today.

The Chocolate Chip Cookie

Depending on who you ask, a historian or a cook, one of the most important inventions at the close of the Industrial Revolution was the chocolate chip cookie. The idea was discovered by Ruth Wakefield of Massachusetts. Ruth was born in 1905 and went to high school, graduating in 1920. She wanted to be a chef, so she attended the Framingham State Normal School Department of Household Arts. After graduating in 1924, she married and started a family, but this did not slow her down.

Ruth and her husband, Kenneth Wakefield, bought a lodge not far from Boston in 1930. In the past, the lodge had been a place for travelers to rest and eat a hot meal. They were also required to pay a toll. Embracing its history, the Wakefields named their business The Toll House Inn, and Ruth cooked for her visiting guests.

According to legend, one night Ruth was baking cookies for her customers and realized she did not have time to melt the large bitter blocks of chocolate used for baking chocolate treats. Instead, she broke up the chocolate into pieces, hoping they would melt into the batter. The tiny chips stayed in place, gooey and hot, and the cookies were a hit.[57]

 FAST FACT The first cookbook published in America was written by a woman, Amelia Simmons, who described herself as an American orphan. Historians believe Amelia was probably a servant from the Hudson Valley region of New York. She titled her book, "American Cookery: or, The Art of Dressing Viands, Fish, Poultry and Vegetables, and the Best Modes of Making Puff-pastes, Pies, Tarts, Puddings, Custards and Preserves, and all kinds of Cakes, from the Imperial Plumb to plain Cake", and published it in 1796. Amelia featured two cookie recipes in her cookbook; one a plain cookie with butter and coriander, and the other, a cookie for Christmas.

57. Lemelson-Mit, 2018

Ruth named her recipe the Toll House Crunch Cookies. They became so popular the recipe was published in newspapers, and Ruth wrote a cookbook that included it. Her cookie recipe helped sales of Nestle chocolate, so the company agreed to print her recipe on their packages and in return, she would be supplied with their chocolate brand for life.

America fell in love with the chocolate chip cookie. They later became a favorite of soldiers during World War II, and the cookies' popularity would spread around the world.

Ruth and her husband retired in 1967 and sold the Toll House Inn. Sadly, it burned to the ground in 1984, but her historic culinary invention lives on.

Anne's Mail Order Catalog

The next time you enjoy flipping through your favorite catalog that arrives in the mailbox, thank Anne Swainson of Chicago, Illinois.

Anne was born in Sweden in 1900. After immigrating to the United States, she pursued an education at the Fine and Applied Arts at Columbia University. After graduating, she went to work at the University of California, Berkeley, teaching textile design and creating ideas for metal housewares for the Chase Revere Copper company.

During this time, catalogs that featured special products for sale by mail order used descriptions, sketches, or wood-cut images. Anne would completely overhaul the catalog into the modern version of what we read today.

In 1931, the dry goods company Montgomery Ward of Chicago hired Anne to start a Bureau of Design for their catalog business that sold household goods. Besides designing some of her own kitchenware, within four years, she had hired 32 designers to invent new products and package them creatively. The inventory ranged from toasters to ovens and refrigerators to toys, electronics, and clothes.

> What was it like to work in a catalog design department in the mid-20th century? Anne wrote an example of what a day at work might be like for her:
>
> > One day's assignment might be a tractor, the next a 10-ton jack. Every beginner learned to draw any kind of ideas fast, accurately, and flawlessly, unless he wished to risk the criticism of a meticulous taskmaster.[58]

Anne was promoted company executive. She was the first woman to oversee other departments at Montgomery Ward during an era when women were expected to work from home instead of an office. Under her direction, Montgomery Ward changed the look of its catalog, which had originally started in 1872. Anne used photographs and color printing and hired models to pose with the products or wear the clothes. Her forward-thinking helped Montgomery Ward survive the Great Depression, open over 600 stores, and compete with the successful Sears catalog for much of the 20th century.

Anne not only opened the door for women in industrial design and management, she pioneered the idea of in-house invention and design within a manufacturing company. Although Montgomery Ward began its decline as a household name after World War II, Anne stayed on with a smaller staff until 1955. She passed away unexpectedly of a heart attack while working in the halls of Montgomery Ward that same year, at the age of 55.

---

58. Veit, 2015

Chapter Ten

Heirlooms of the Industrial Age

Antique furniture, china dishes, and gemstone jewelry are often passed down from one generation to the next as precious family heirlooms. Just like these treasures that remind us of the past, the Industrial Revolution remains a historical marker in history that changed the lives of Americans, especially women, who enjoy the fruits of our ancestors' labors and dreams.

The Industrial Revolution taught mankind innumerous valuable lessons, from science to politics, to lessons of economy and equality. It was a tipping point of economic growth and opportunity. We've learned from the tapping of natural resources that finding ways to meet our basic needs fuels inventions. Consider the explosion of the coal industry in pre-Industrial Revolution Great Britain. This basic resource was so plentiful it became affordable. People were able to keep warm and cook their food. Steam engines were invented or improved, and, eventually, locomotives and ships puffed their way around the world.

Resources and inventions fuel economies and trade. During the Industrial Revolution, Great Britain became the world's most powerful empire. The United States built cities and expanded its reach west. By the time of the World Wars, the countries were allies in the defense of world peace. Prosperity as a result of industrialization created opportunities for education, employment, and advancements in social class.

What else has the Industrial Revolution taught us? Mark Hutchinson of daily online magazine, The Globalist said, "…it is important to be the very best — or the very cheapest. Mediocrity and average performance win no prizes in economic development…"[59]

Is there a hard lesson? Perhaps one of the biggest messages of the Age of Machines is the dangers of greed and inequality. Workers, including women and children, suffered during those early days under sometimes barbaric conditions. It was an opportunity for wages, but came at the great cost to health or life. The outcry against these practices, and the sacrifices made by early unions and women's rights advocates spurred on the idea of equality of all Americans, a foundation for women's suffrage and, even later, the Civil Rights Movement.

 Although women are on track for full equality in the workforce, women still earned only 82 percent of what men made in 2017.[60]

One may argue that women are the biggest winners of the American Industrial Revolution. Where they were once seen as having no potential beyond working as a servant or artisan, they are now considered equal to men in ability and intelligence. The granddaughters of the Industrial Revolution pioneered scientific advances, invented new technologies, managed companies and corporations, and continue to work beside their male counterparts, leading fields that are now changing the landscape of America in technology and engineering.

Progressive Women Now

Another one of the "heirlooms" of the Industrial Revolution are the types jobs available to women today. We live in the era of technology, a period

---

59. Hutchinson, 2009
60. Bls.gov, 2018

that exploded during the 1950s and 1960s when computers became a reality and man walked on the moon. Rather than walking into dusty, oily factories with loud clanking machines and afflicted workers, we are surrounded by artificial intelligences at the dawn of another transformation, the 21st Century Data Revolution.

Tracking with Tesla

Whether or not you are old enough to drive a car, you have probably heard of Tesla. It is an electric car that takes advantage of battery packs and solar-powered engineering. Meredith Westafer is the senior industrial engineer with Tesla Motors and was featured as one of Business Insiders' Most Powerful Female Engineers of 2018.

Meredith works in design, managing the company's Gigafactory, which supplies the lithium-ion batteries needed for Tesla products. Her job involves working with space and operations' flow among the automated robots working on a production line. Located in Nevada, it is expected to soon be the world's largest operating factory — with a woman at the wheel.

Alice Zhang

Entrepreneur Alice Zhang formed her own drug company, Verge Genomics, after leaving the PhD program at UCLA (University of California Los Angeles) in 2015. The mission of the company is to combine academics with computers and industry to better understand diseases and to discover new drugs to treat them. One of the first goals for this accomplished woman is to tackle neurodegenerative illnesses like **Parkinson's disease**. Forbes named Alice Zhang as one to watch in their 2017 "Thirty Under 30" list of young innovators.[61]

---

61. Knapp, 2017

Microsoft's mathematician

Another woman advancing the technological field at Microsoft is Krysta Svore. She is the principle research manager with a leading computer company, working with **quantum** algorithms that may one day create a computer faster than any that are known today.

Growing up, Krysta attended an all-girls school in Washington State. She credits her work and success to the women who taught and mentored her in science and math. At her day job, this super scientist works with numbers, code, and hardware platforms to drive the insides of super computers.

Lori Greiner

Millions of Americans purchase goods from television advertisements, and the QVC network is king of the home shopping channels. One of the most successful women in retail ever is Lori Greiner, who features her inventions on television so successfully that she is known as the "Queen of QVC."

Lori invented an earring organizer in 1996 and decided to patent and produce it herself. She soon figured out the ropes of marketing and advertising and became so successful that she organized her own company, For Your Ease Only. She has invented over 500 retail household items and has a regular guest job on the popular entrepreneurial show "Shark Tank." As of 2017, Lori's business ventures were valued at over $50 million.[62]

---

62. Knight, 2017

Progressive power

Another notable woman making a difference in the world is Jessica Matthews. A duel citizen of both the United States and Nigeria, Jessica graduated from Harvard University. During her time at university, she studied new solutions for problems in developing and was on a team that created a soccer ball that stored motion-action energy, or **kinetic energy,** as it was kicked around. The stored energy in the soccer ball could be used if electricity was not available to light lamps or flashlights after dark.

Smithsonian Magazine named Jessica as one of its "Ten Female Innovators to Watch In 2018" for founding her own company, Uncharted Power.[63] The company's mission is to make energy convenient in every location around the world. Uncharted Power takes advantage of the kinetic energy concept, like storing energy in sidewalks that is produced when people walk over them. At the time this book was written, Uncharted Power had 10 global patents pending and was exploring other renewable energy options in at least 10 different countries around the world.

Whether they are working from home, in their communities, or leading the charge in different industries, progressive women continue to lead the way. By studying and reading up on current events happening around us, we can discover and support women who are providing leadership and inspiration for the next generation.

The Future Looks Bright

So what lies ahead for American industry? How will it affect society and women? The future looks bright.

---

63. Matchar, 2018

The technology revolution brought us the internet, and today it a part of nearly everyone's life, whether for work, staying connected to the world, or networking with friends on social media.

The internet has revolutionized American jobs, business, society, and even our culture. Information and communication are literally at our fingertips, and we can access both at the speed of light.

 An artificial intelligence company in Hungary has invented self-driving cars that use six onboard cameras with computer algorithms. The company, Almotive, believes it can improve safety. If successful, it would change traditional car manufacturing jobs and the driving experience as we know it.

As the new century plunges us forward into the Data Revolution, we can expect to continue seeing amazing education and business opportunities formed from data gathered in real time from micro to macro levels; in other words, from the cell structure of a fatal disease to the reproduction and migration patterns of whales in the sea and birds in the skies.

 A clean-tech company, Enevo, is based in Finland and has created a trash disposal company that uses data to maximize savings and efficiency. Orange sensors on trash cans and dumpsters provide the company's trash collectors with information that helps them plan fuel and time-efficient schedules and routes. Enevo made over $3 million in 2016 and plans to expand its reach to America.[64]

Revolutions change us. The invention of the telescope in 1586 and the microscope in 1650 certainly affected how man saw the world and himself. Cars and airplanes made transportation faster and more convenient. Computers connected us to information and one another. All of it has brought about great

---

64. Peterson, 2018

change, a modification of human perception, or how we think. And changing the way we think is how new doors are opened and worlds discovered.

 Some are single, some are married, and some are mothers, but over 40 percent of women in the workforce have college degrees.

Today, women are not only a part of these amazing discoveries, but they are an integral part of the American workforce. Since World War II, the number of working American women has gone up from 38 to 57 percent.[65] As of 2017, there were over 74 million women with jobs, making females 47 percent of the American workforce.[66] According to accounting receipts, women own almost 10 million U.S. businesses.[67]

 There are 774 million illiterate people in the world and 2/3 of them are women.[68]

About 116 million women in developing countries never completed primary school.[69]

About 14 percent of the global population does not have access to electricity.[70]

Where once America was a small group of dependent colonies, it is now a world leader in women' rights and education. More and more women can now provide mentorship for those less fortunate around them, as well as serve as examples of the power of women and industry to others in developing countries and other nations. In the future, literacy and opportuni-

65. DeWolf, 2017
66. Ibid
67. Ibid
68. UNESCO.org, 2013
69. Ibid
70. Iea.org, 2018

ties in the workforce may finally equalize the numbers between men and women in the United States and around the world. Let's change the world.

Steam engines, clockworks, quirky inventions, and loud, clacking factories. These images are the symbols of the Industrial Revolution era. Why does this period in world history matter so much to us today? Why should we remember it? Study it?

As mentioned in the final chapter of this book, the technological advances that sparked the beginnings of the Industrial Revolution brought us to where we are today. We owe our forbearers who pioneered the fields of math, science, and politics a debt of gratitude for opening doors to new ideas and inventions that allowed everyone, especially women and the lower classes, a chance for a better life.

Today, the industry and the production of goods provide for the needs and wants in our society through jobs still centered around factories, although times have changed. In the United States and other developed countries, gone now are small children scurrying under rickety machines. They have been replaced by conveyor belts and robots. Employees who still work in factories no longer slave away for 14 hours a day or more at a backbreaking, inhumane pace but instead work with computers and machines. Detailed or artisan work by hand is controlled by safety regulations, and workers can expect better work shifts and pay than the pioneer factory weavers had in times past.

Yes, there are giant corporations like Amazon or Walmart that rule certain industries, but competition helps keep prices fair and work conditions for their employees in compliance with laws and workers' rights. Whether it is food service, home improvement centers, or product production lines, there are millions of jobs working in warehouses with forklifts and pallets, or maintaining customer service by handling sales both online and in person at brick and mortar stores. Even car manufacturer employees assembling automobiles use modern technology while enjoying salaries and benefits, like discounts on the company cars they build, that help maintain a competitive and comfortable lifestyle.

The evolution of our machine revolution did not just change how we work. It lit the sparks for other battles in social class, racial equality, and women's rights. Over time, it provided opportunities for class advancement in our society. Where one generation worked in early century factories or farmed, the next pursued education or employment opportunities in the improved work force of industrial jobs. Better jobs and better pay meant even more opportunities for higher education and exclusive careers once only available to the higher classes, usually white males, in decades past. Today, companies and organizations focus on diversity and equality as they consider the best employees for their available jobs.

Women, too, owe those first gritty, determined factory girls a great deal of respect and gratitude. Their early sacrifices fanned the flames of gender equality and provided evidence that anything he can do, she can do just as well. As women's rights and respect for gender makes progress in the United States, it continues to develop around the world.

Today's new revolution in the fields of technology and data can change life for the better for future generations, and that can be our legacy. Our new age of computers and networking provides additional advantages and opportunities that are now open to women and minorities. Most importantly, those who embrace invention and progress can stand as role models and mentors to others around the world still fighting for change.

I love my tablet. I enjoy trips to the movies, my time-keeping cell phone, and especially my little blue Prius that takes me where I want to go. Almost all of the everyday tools I have at my disposal, including my freedom to work and express myself, I owe to the Industrial Revolution.

And so do you.

When the opportunity came to write a book about our past that laid its groundwork when Queen Victoria ruled, I could not pass up the chance. Between the shiny gadgets and strong women using fashion, politics, and literature to assert their independence, the Industrial Revolution was truly the dawn of an era that changed mankind and affected our destiny.

For me, discovering the roots of America's role in the Industrial Revolution was a journey of discovery, reminders, and *ah-ha* moments. I hope there were some for you, too.

As an author, half the joy of writing history is the research. This means a great deal of time looking through books, searching magazine and scholarly articles online, and the best part — pictures.

Thank goodness for even the primitive days of photography that captured so many moments of the past, whether it was working in the first factories, protesting in the streets, or selling those first amazing, life-changing inventions. I invite you to not only read good books about history, but to study the pictures and sketches of artists and photographers that have been catalogued online or are illustrated in this book. History, after all, is really about the individuals who make it.

So, the next time you are introduced to an innovative new idea or invention, I hope you will remember what you learned between the pages of this book. I hope you will recall the first brave inventors and thinkers in America, as well as those early savvy business men and women who improved the quality and speed of production to supply our demand for new things. Most importantly, never forget those who fought for fairness and equality.

New ideas can become great things, and those great things can eventually make life better for all of us. These stories should not be forgotten. Because of the Industrial Revolution in America, we can muster up our own courage, pursue our own dreams, and fight for what we believe is good, better, best… and right.

Glossary

4-H: a global network of youth organizations that teaches life skills, responsibility, and hard work

Abolitionist: a protestor of slavery and other inequalities

Admiral Charles Stewart: an officer born in 1778 who served in the United States Navy and commanded a number of U.S. Navy ships, including the famous *USS Constitution*

Agriculture: farming the land and raising livestock

Armory: a room or building to store weapons

Artisans: a worker in a skilled trade who usually makes things by hand

Atlantic Slave Trade: the transportation and commerce of enslaved African people from the 16th to 19th centuries

Bayonet: a sword attached to the end of a rifle

Blacklisted: to be avoided, ignored, or boycotted, usually by employers

Boarding keepers: men or women who run a boarding house and watch over the residents

Bobbins: a cylinder that holds thread, wire, yarn, or other strings

Boston Manufacturing Company: the first factory company formed in the United States

Campfire Girls: a co-ed youth development organization that emphasizes outdoor activities for youth

Columbia Paper Bag Company: an early paper bag factory located in Springfield, Massachusetts

Compensation: payment to someone for work, loss, or suffering

Cottage industry :a home business

Cotton gin: a machine that separates cotton seeds from cotton

Daguerreotypes: a photographic process that uses an iodine-sensitized silvered plate and a mercury vapor to produce an image

Dead Letter Office: a facility within a postal system where undeliverable mail is processed

Doffers: industrial factory workers who replaced bobbins or other supplies on the weaving machines

Domestic manufacture: a household's skills and labor; a country's own goods rather than imported products.

Economic Game Company: a New York game company formed by Elizabeth Magie and E. H. Monroe of Chicago and E. G. Lenbusher of New York in 1906

Eastern Paper Bag Company: the 1870 paper bag company founded by Margaret Knight, inventor of the folded paper bag.

Executors: lawyers

Erie Canal: the canal built to connect Lake Erie to the Hudson and Buffalo Rivers in New York

Forgery: a fake or copy made with the intention to deceive

Flying shuttle: a weaving machine on wheels within a track that used paddles to move the shuttle from side to side by pulling a cord

Gilded Age: a time of rapid economic growth and great wealth for members of the upper classes

Girl Scouts: a youth organization for girls in the United States and American girls living abroad that teaches life skills

Guilds: medieval associations of craftsmen

Hernia: when an internal organ pushes out through a weak spot in the body cavity

Inequality: imbalance, inconsistency

Indentured servants: a person who is bound by a contract to work for a fixed time

Industrial revolution: the age of power and the mechanization of agriculture and textile

Interest: money paid at a percentage rate for the use of money borrowed

Jeannette Pickering Rankin: the first woman to hold federal office (1916) in the United States

Jeffersonians: those who followed a type of democracy with Republican values; named after Thomas Jefferson

John Fitch: an American inventor and engineer born in 1783 in Connecticut who is remembered for operating the first steamboat service in the United States

John J. Cisco & Son: a famous banking institution in the late 19th century located on Wall Street

Kevlar: a strong and heat-resistant fiber first used in the 1970s as a replacement for steel in tires and later developed for use into other products for strength and protection

Kinetic energy: the amount of work needed to accelerate a body from rest to a velocity

Kitchen Aid: an American appliance brand of standing mixers started in 1919 by the Hobart Corporation; owned by Whirlpool Corporation today

Knight-Davidson Motor Company: a company that produced automobiles with the K-D engine invented by Margaret Knight; also known as the K-D Motor Company

Living wage: the minimum income necessary for basic needs

Loom: a contraption for making fabric by weaving yarn or thread in rows

Lowell Female Labor Reform Association (LFLRA): the first union of American working women ever formed

Newcomen steam engine: an engine invented by Thomas Newcomen in 1712 that operated by condensing steam in a cylinder to push a piston into a cylinder

Manufactories: factories

Manufacturing: the production of merchandise using labor, machines, tools, and forms of processing

Marie Curie: the Polish-French physicist and chemist who pioneered radioactivity research

MIT: Massachusetts Institute of Technology; a private-research school in Cambridge, Massachusetts

Mortgages: a loan of money, usually in large sums, used to buy real estate and that call for a percentage fee to paid back with the loan

National Inventors Hall of Fame: an American organization that recognizes engineers and inventors who hold a U.S. patent for significant technology

National Museum of American History: a nationally run museum in Washington D.C. that collects and exhibits items of social, political, cultural, scientific, and military importance

Panic of 1907: a U.S. financial crisis that took place over a three-week period in October of 1907 when the New York Stock Exchange fell almost 50 percent

Parker Brothers: an American toy company formed in 1883 by George Swinnerton Parker in Pawtucket, Rhode Island, and later bought by Hasbro

Parkinson's Disease: a nervous system disorder that affects muscle movement

Patent: an exclusive right granted for an invention

Petition: a formal request to authority signed by any number of people

Phosphorous: the chemical element symbol P with the atomic number 15; a highly reactive element

Piecer: a factory worker who leaned over the spinning-machine to repair the broken threads

Pitt saw: a large saw with handles at each end used by two people, with one standing above the timber to be cut, the other in a pit below it

Polonium: the chemical element Po with the atomic number 84; a rare and highly radioactive metal

Polyamides: the linkage of an amino group of one molecule and a carboxylic acid group of another to create an artificial polymer

Polymers: a large molecule composed of many repeated subunits

Protocol of Peace: a historic compromise between the International Ladies Garment Workers Union and the garment industry in New York City

Prototype: an early model of something that will later be developed

Pyrotechnic: the science of using chemical material to produce heat, light, gas, smoke, and/or sound

Quaker Westtown School: a boarding school in West Chester, Pennsylvania formed in 1799

Quantum: energy equal in magnitude to the frequency of the radiation it represents

Radiation: energy in the form of waves or particles that travel through space or materials

Radium: the silvery-white chemical element Ra with the atomic number 88

Ramrods: a rod used to ram down the charge into the muzzle of a musket or other firearm

Rhode Island Factory System: a system of mills built around small villages and farms and other resources needed to support a population

Royal Legion of Honor: an award presented by England for military or excellent civil service; France has its own version, too.

Seneca Falls Convention: the first women's rights convention in the United States; conducted in 1848 in Seneca Falls, New York

Sleeve valve engine: a type of valve mechanism for piston engines

Spinning jenny: a machine that spins and uses more than one spindle

Stenographer: a person who transcribes speech into a brief form of handwriting called shorthand or longhand.

Strike: when workers organize and refuse to work or be productive on the job

Strokes: when blood flow in the brain is cut off

Textiles: fabric, cloth, and other production materials

Syphilis: a bacterial infection caused by intimate contact

Underground Railroad: secret routes and safe houses used by African-American slaves to escape to the North during the early to mid-19th century and Civil War

Unions: an organization of workers who come together to achieve goals

United States Radium Corporation: formed from the Radium Luminous Material Corporation in 1914 in Orange, New Jersey

War bonds: notes issued by a government to finance military operations

Watt steam engine: the first steam engine to use a separate condenser so as not to waste steam energy

Wilhem Conrad Roentgen: the German mechanical engineer and physicist who discovered electromagnetic radiation waves (X-rays) and earned the Nobel Prize in Physics in 1901

Wrought nails: nails made entirely by hand

Bibliography

1. Newman, Simon P. "'In Great Slavery and Bondage': White Labor and the Development of Plantation Slavery in British America," in Gallup-Diaz, Ignacio, Shankman, Andrew, and Silverman, David J., eds. *Anglicizing America : Empire, Revolution, Republic* (Philadelphia: University of Pennsylvania Press, 2015).

2. The Editors of Encyclopaedia Britannica. "Water Frame." Encyclopædia Britannica. https://www.britannica.com/technology/water-frame. 30 November 2017. Web. August 2018.

3. Frader, Laura L. *The Industrial Revolution: A History in Documents.* Oxford University Press; 1 edition (April 6, 2006).

4. "Native Americans." CPRR Discussion Group. Central Pacific Railroad Photographic History Museum. http://discussion.cprr.net/2009/09/native-americans.html. 14 September 2009. Web. October 2018.

5. Frader, Laura L. The Industrial Revolution: A History in Documents. Oxford University Press; 1 edition (April 6, 2006).

6. Avery, John. "Life at Lowell Mills. Factory Rules from the Handbook to Lowell, 1848." The Illinois Labor History Society. http://www.kentlaw.edu/ilhs/lowell.htm. Web. August 2018.

7. Avery, John. "Life at Lowell Mills. Factory Rules from the Handbook to Lowell, 1848." The Illinois Labor History Society. http://www.kentlaw.edu/ilhs/lowell.htm. Web. August 2018.

8. Avery John. "Life at Lowell Mills. Factory Rules from the Handbook to Lowell, 1848." The Illinois Labor History Society. http://www.kentlaw.edu/ilhs/lowell.htm. Web. August 2018.

9. Robinson, Harriet. "The Characteristics of the Early Factory Girls." *Loom and Spindle; or, Life among the Early Mill Girls.* 1898.

10. "Life at Lowell Mills." The Illinois Labor History Society. https://www.umbc.edu/che/tahlessons/pdf/Methods_of_Reform_The_Lowell_Mill_Girls_RS_3.pdf. Web. October 2018.

11. "Life at Lowell Mills." The Illinois Labor History Society. https://www.umbc.edu/che/tahlessons/pdf/Methods_of_Reform_The_Lowell_Mill_Girls_RS_3.pdf. Web. October 2018.

12. Orestes, A. Brownson. *The Laboring Classes: An Article from the Boston Quarterly Review*, Boston: Benjamin H. Greene, 1840, page 11.

13. Robinson, Harriet. "The Characteristics of the Early Factory Girls." Loom and Spindle; or, Life among the Early Mill Girls. 1898.

14. Howe, Walker Daniel. What Hath God Wrought: The Transformation of America, 1815-1848. Oxford University Press, 2007.

15. "Turnout in Lowell." Boston Transcript. 1834. http://connectsemass.org/. Web. October 2018.

16. "Lowell Mill Women Create the First Union of Working Women." AFL-CIO., America's Unions. https://aflcio.org/. Web. October 2018.

17. de Safita, Neathery. "A Brief History Of Paper." July 2002. St. Louis Community College. http://users.stlcc.edu/nfuller/paper/. Web. October 2018.

18. Hanaford, Phebe Ann. *Women of the Century*. Nabu Press, 2011.

19. Meares, Hadley. "The invention of the paper bag was a triumph of feminism." 30 May 2016. Aeon. https://aeon.co/. Web. October 2018.

20. "The American Package Museum." *The American Package Museum*, www.packagemuseum.com/. Web. October 2018.

21. Savchuk, Katia. "America's Oldest Billion-Dollar Family Fortunes." 1 July 2015. Forbes.com. Web. September 2016.

22. Boston Post. 20 March 1902. Obituary. https://www.newspapers.com/clip/22231928/edward_henry_green18211902_obituary/. Web. October 2018.

23. Laneri, Raquel. "Why Wall Street's 'witch' was actually a woman to be admired." 8 August 2018. Nypost.com. Web. September 2018.

24. O Henry. "The Skylight Room." 1906. Americanliterature.com. Web. September 2018.

25. Slack, Charles. *Hetty: The Genius and Madness of America's First Female Tycoon. Harper Collins 2011*

26. Pilon, Mary. "Monopoly's Inventor: The Progressive Who Didn't Pass 'Go'". 13 February 2015. Nytimes.com. Web. September 2018.

27. Pilon, Mary. "Monopoly's Inventor: The Progressive Who Didn't Pass 'Go'". 13 February 2015. Nytimes.com. Web. September 2018.same

28. Pilon, Mary. "Monopoly's Inventor: The Progressive Who Didn't Pass 'Go'". 13 February 2015. Nytimes.com. Web. September 2018.same

29. Miller, Joseph Dana. *Land and Freedom: An International Record of Single Tax Progress, Volume 2.* 15 July 1902.

30. Miller, Joseph Dana. Land and Freedom: An International Record of Single Tax Progress, Volume 2. 15 July 1902.

31. Miller, Joseph Dana. Land and Freedom: An International Record of Single Tax Progress, Volume 2. 15 July 1902.

32. The Single Tax Review, Autumn 1902.

33. Dodson, Edward J. "How Henry George's Principles Were Corrupted Into the Game Called Monopoly." December 2011. www.henry-george.org. Web. September 2016.

34. Dodson, Edward J. "How Henry George's Principles Were Corrupted Into the Game Called Monopoly." December 2011. www.henrygeorge.org. Web. September 2016.

35. Magie, Elizabeth. "A Word to the Wise." *Land and Freedom.* September-October. 1940.

36. Miller, Stephen M. *Inspired Innovations: A Celebration of Shaker Ingenuity.* University Press of New England, New Hampshire: 2010.

37. Coston, Martha J. *A Signal Success: The Work and Travels of Mrs. Martha J. Coston.* J.B. Lippencott Company, 1886.

38. Coston, Martha J. A Signal Success: The Work and Travels of Mrs. Martha J. Coston. J.B. Lippencott Company, 1886.same

39. Coston, Martha J. A Signal Success: The Work and Travels of Mrs. Martha J. Coston. J.B. Lippencott Company, 1886.same

40. "Facts and Figures." Mta.info. *web.mta.info/nyct/facts/ffsubway.htm* Web. September 2018.

41. Walton, M.B. US237422A. 1881. Patents.google.com. Web. September 2018.

42. Walton, M.B. US237422A. 1881. Patents.google.com. Web. September 2018

43. Engineering.com. "Mary Walton." 12 October 2006. Web. September 2018.

44. From Sur Une Nouvelle Substance Fortement Radio-Active, Contenue Dans La Pitchblende by M. P. Curie, Mme. P. Curie and M. G. Bemont, Comptes rendus, Vol 127, Dec 1898.

45. From Sur Une Nouvelle Substance Fortement Radio-Active, Contenue Dans La Pitchblende by M. P. Curie, Mme. P. Curie and M. G. Bemont, Comptes rendus, Vol 127, Dec 1898.

46. Moore, Kate. *The Radium Girls.* Illinois: Sourcebook, Inc., 2017.

47. Moore, Kate. *The Radium Girls.* Illinois: Sourcebook, Inc., 2017.

48. Moore, Kate. *The Radium Girls.* Illinois: Sourcebook, Inc., 2017.

49. Swanson, Eleanor. "Radium Girls." The Missouri Review. 1 March 2002.

50. "Women in Unions." Institute for Women's Policy Research. https://iwpr.org/. Web. October 2018.

51. "Time Line: Women in the U.S. Military." The Colonial Williamsburg Foundation. 2008. History.org. Web. October 2018.

52. History.com Editors. "Harriet Beecher Stowe." A&E Television Networks. https://www.history.com/topics/american-civil-war/harriet-beecher-stowe. 12 November 2009. Web. October 2018.

53. Medina, Jason. Kings Park Psychiatric Center: a Journey Through History: Volume 1. Xlibris, 2018.

54. "Jeanette Rankin." History, Art, & Archives, United States House of Representatives. https://history.house.gov/. Web. October 2018.

55. "Diaper Facts." Real Diaper Association. http://realdiapers.org/diaper-facts. 2004-2014. Web. October 2018.

56. "Stephanie L. Kwolek." Science History Institute. https://www.sciencehistory.org. 9 December 2017. Web. October 2018.

57. "Ruth Wakefield: Toll House Chocolate Chip Cookies." Lemelson-Mit. http://lemelson.mit.edu/resources/ruth-wakefield. Web. December 2018.

58. Veit, Rebecca. "Anne Swainson, Founder of America's First Corporate ID Department And inventor of the modern mail-order catalog." Core77.com. 15 September 2015. Web.   October 2018.

59. Hutchinson, Martin. "Lessons from the Industrial Revolution." Theglobalist.com. 2 December 2009. Web. October 2018.

60. "Highlights of women's earnings in 2017." U.S. Bureau of Labor Statistics. Report 1075. https://www.bls.gov/opub/reports/womens-earnings/2017/pdf/home.pdf. Web. October   2018.

61. Knapp, Alex. "30 Under 30 in Science 2017: Discovering New Things About Our Own World And New Ways To Save It." Forbes.com. 3 Jan 2017. Web. December 2018.

62. Knight, Cheryl. "Lori Greiner's net worth is $50 million." Celebrity Money. https://www.bankrate.com. 24 April 2017. Web. October 2017.

63. Matchar, Emily. "Ten Female Innovators to Watch In 2018." Smithsonian.com. 27 March 2018. Web. December 2018.

64. Peterson, Becky. "Snowflake's CEO shares how he got a $1.5 billion valuation from Sequoia Capital just four years out of stealth mode." https://nordic.businessinsider.com/. 30 January 2018. Web. October 2018.

65. DeWolf, Mark. "12 Stats About Working Women." U.S. Department of Labor Blog. https://blog.dol.gov/2017/03/01/12-stats-about-working-women. 1 March 2017. Web. October 2018.

66. DeWolf, Mark. "12 Stats About Working Women." U.S. Department of Labor Blog. https://blog.dol.gov/2017/03/01/12-stats-about-working-women. 1 March 2017. Web.   October 2018.

67. DeWolf, Mark. "12 Stats About Working Women." U.S. Department of Labor Blog. https://blog.dol.gov/2017/03/01/12-stats-about-working-women. 1 March 2017. Web. October 2018.

68. "Education for All Global Monitoring Report, Girls' Education—the facts." Fact Sheet EFA GMR's World Inequality Database in Education (WIDE). https://en.unesco.org/. October 2013. Web. October 2018.

69. "Education for All Global Monitoring Report, Girls' Education—the facts." Fact Sheet EFA GMR's World Inequality Database in Education (WIDE). https://en.unesco.org/. October 2013. Web. October 2018.

70. Energy access database. International Energy Agency. https://www.iea.org/energyaccess/database/. Web. October 2018.

Index

Danielle Thorne is the author of over a dozen books. When she is not traveling, reading, or streaming videos, she writes historical fiction and non-fiction, along with other genres, for all ages. A graduate of BYU-Idaho, Danielle lives south of Atlanta, Georgia with her husband, youngest son, and orange tabby. Besides writing pursuits that include a paranormal series, she's judged writing contests and edited fiction for Solstice and Desert Breeze Publishing. You can connect with Danielle on social media sites such as Facebook, Twitter, and Instagram.

Find more of Danielle's books on Amazon.com.

Made in the USA
Middletown, DE
14 September 2022